Orchids

I. D. James

FIREFLY BOOKS

Acknowledgments: The author wishes to thank L & R Orchids, Ron Maunder and Val Bayliss for their assistance, together with the many growers who allowed their plants to be photographed.

Photographic Credits: Val Bayliss pages 1,13,16,17,21,25,28,29,30,36,58,66,80,81,84,88,89.
Selwyn Hatrick pages 10,24,65,74,75,77,78,79.
Dr John Feltwell, Garden & Wildlife Matters Photo Library pages 23,85.
Remaining photographs by author.

Drawings: Gillian James

Page 1: *Masdevallia* Gertrude Puttock. Several plants raised from the same seed capsule.

Page 2: *Miltonia* Snowqualmie

Page 3: *Disa* Riette

A FIREFLY BOOK c(0 HH VG

Published by Firefly Books Ltd. 2001

First Printing 2001, reprinted 2003.

Library of Congress Cataloging in Publication Data is available.

Canadian Cataloguing in Publication Data

James, I.D.
    Orchids

Includes index.

ISBN 1-55209-569-X (bound) ISBN 1-55209-508-8 (pbk.)

1. Orchid culture. 2. Orchids. I. Title

SB409.J35 2001 635.9'344 C00-931747-3

Published in the United States in 2001 by Firefly Books (U.S.) Inc.
P.O. Box 1338, Ellicott Station, Buffalo, New York 14205

Published in Canada in 2001 by Firefly Books Ltd.
3680 Victoria Park Avenue, Willowdale, Ontario M2H 3K1

Visit our website at www.fireflybooks.com

Cover design by Shelley Watson, Sublime Design
Book design by Errol McLeary
Typesetting by Jazz Graphics
Printed in China through Colorcraft Ltd., Hong Kong

Contents

Introduction

The orchid is the most highly evolved of all the plant families. Our attraction to them has been suggested as a natural one between the most highly evolved plant and the most highly evolved animal – human beings.

There are probably over 25,000 different species growing in the wild, making the orchid one of the largest, if not the largest, plant family. To this figure can be added over 100,000 cultivated hybrids. The vast majority of these have been raised over the last 50 years but many seem to have been eventually discarded and are no longer in collections. The species can be found growing in suitable locations everywhere outside of the Arctic and Antarctic, although even here there are exceptions with a few even growing inside the Arctic Circle. Only a fraction of the known species are currently being cultivated by orchid growers.

Orchids that prefer to grow on the branches of trees are termed **epiphytes** (*epi*, from the Greek *upon*, and *phyte* from the Greek *phuton*, for plant). Those found on rock faces are **lithophytic** ("stone-plant") or **rupicolous** ("rock-dwelling"). Many grow in the soil like ordinary garden plants and are said to be **terrestrial**. Some cultivated orchids loosely referred to as being terrestrial have their roots in the litter on top of the forest floor rather than in the soil. Epiphytes and lithophytes are plants of tropical and sub-tropical rainforests, and it is here that are found the greatest number and greatest diversity of orchid. Further away from the equator, most or all the orchids in nature will be true terrestrials. Some of these are very difficult to cultivate if removed from their natural environment are best left to be enjoyed where they are.

Opposite: *Cattleya* Rivermont Imperial 'Gamma'

It is not always easy to identify a plant as an orchid if it is not in flower. Orchids come in a diversity of shapes and sizes. The growth habit can be **monopodial**, such as in *Vanda*, where a single stem grows upward forever or until some accident damages the growing tip and then a new shoot may be initiated near the bottom of the plant. Alternatively, orchids can be **sympodial**, as in *Cattleya*, where a new growth is produced each year from the base of the previous one. Sympodial orchids typically have swollen stems as storage organs. Where the entire length of the stem is evenly swollen, as in many *Dendrobium*, this is called a **cane**. The swollen bulb-like base, as in *Cymbidium*, is called a **pseudobulb**, but these come in many shapes and sizes in different genera. Some terrestrial orchids have underground tubers as storage organs. The roots of epiphytic orchids are encased in thick layers of water-absorbing cells called the **velamen**. Apart from the growing tip, the velamen is dead tissue. Although the tissue is dead, it should not be allowed to decay, otherwise the live conducting tissues in the center may perish also.

Orchids are **monocotyledons**, where the flower parts are arranged in groups of three or multiples of three. The orchid flower has three **sepals** (the parts visible in an unopened flower bud) and three **petals**. One of the petals is modified in shape and often color and this is the **labellum** or lip. In some species these parts can show considerable variation in size, shape and form, sometimes to the extent that to the uninitiated they do not look like orchid flowers. Unlike other flowering plants where the stamens bearing pollen and the stigma that receives the pollen are on separate organs, in the orchid all these sexual parts are typically all borne on a fleshy structure called the **column**. If the flower has this prominent organ, then it must be an orchid.

From the point of view of the orchid, the sole purpose of the floral display is the attraction and then the manipulation of a pollinator. The pollinating insect may be attracted to the flower from a distance by scent. The flowers of many species resemble insects. In *Ophrys* the flower not only looks like the insect but emits a scent similar to that of the female of the species. The male is attracted by the scent, deceived by the look of the flower, attempts to copulate and transfers pollen from the previous plant that received its attention. There are species of *Bulbophyllum* that are pollinated by flies and have the scent of rotting flesh.

In many orchids the insect lands on the lip, a convenient landing platform. The pollen from the flower previously visited is on its back and in forcing its way between the lip and the column, it deposits the pollen on the sticky stigmatic surface on the underside of the column. The insect's goal is to reach nectar in a spur at the base of the lip. The process is aided by the fact that unlike the loose pollen of other flowers, the pollen in most orchids is aggregated into solid discrete packages called **pollinia**. In backing out the insect unhinges the pollinia under a cap at the end of the column and carries this off to the next flower. Self-pollination is thus unlikely, something most, but not all, orchids strive to avoid to ensure genetic diversity in the progeny.

The variation in orchid flowers and their pollination mechanisms seems never-ending. The first person to draw attention to these was Charles Darwin in the middle of the 19th century in his work "The Various Contrivances by which Orchids are Fertilised by Insects".

To give but two further examples, there are flowers, such as in *Paphiopedilum*, where the lip is modified to form a pouch into which the insect falls and is trapped. The only way to get out is up a ladder of hairs and the route to freedom forces the insect to deposit and remove pollinia. Then there are orchids, such as *Catasetum*, which do not rely on a passive approach, as they literally fire the pollinia at the insect. It will fire it at you, too, if you touch the sensitive trigger mechanism.

Some orchid flowers are so constructed that only one species of insect is able to gain the access necessary for pollination. One wonders just what the effect would be on either of these life forms if one became extinct for some reason. There are orchids, usually with red or orange flowers, that are pollinated by birds – usually birds capable of hovering like hummingbirds. However pollinated, the floral parts in most orchids (but not the column or ovary) die when pollinated. Unless pollinated, most orchid species will have reasonably long-lasting flowers. On the other hand, *Diplocaulobium* flowers last but a single day. At the other end of the spectrum is *Dendrobium cuthbertsonii*, a miniature species found at high altitudes in Irian Jaya and Papua New Guinea. The brilliantly colored flowers of this species last for no less than six months. This unusual longevity suggests that the plant may be visited only infrequently by a pollinator.

In the early days of orchid culture, growers did not have a lot of success until they became aware of the conditions in which various species were found in nature and attempted to duplicate them in the greenhouse. Latitude alone is not a reliable guide. Lowland tropical rainforests are not rich in orchid flora, although some important cultivated orchids originate there. One must usually climb above sea level before finding orchids in abundance and this abundance can continue up to beyond 6560 ft (2000 m). In tropical rainforests near the equator, such as in New Guinea, there is a rich and diverse population well above 9840 ft (3000 m) and that is a long way up.

At very high elevations orchids do not experience very high maximum temperatures and these may fall at night low enough to cause frost on open areas outside the forest canopy. The plants may be subject to daily rain or cloud envelopment and strong sunlight intense in the UV spectrum. It will be apparent that we cannot successfully grow all kinds of orchids from all climates under exactly the same conditions. Many growers choose to specialize in those kinds that do well for them in the particular growing environment they are able to provide.

Hardiness Zones

The world has been divided into plant hardiness zones. They are based on the lowest temperature recorded in each year over the period records have been kept. They are air temperatures taken above ground level not frost recordings. In the USA they are read from a thermometer about 6 ft (2 m) above the ground.

The zones can be useful in indicating the kinds of orchids that might be grown in your area in the shade of a tree in the garden, in a shade-house, or an unheated enclosed greenhouse. Where orchids are in an artificially heated greenhouse or in the home the zones do not limit what can be grown and are only relevant when considering the amount of heating necessary to maintain the minimum temperatures required.

Minimum temperatures are only one segment of the growing environment. The climate zones do not provide any information about maximum temperatures and there are some cool-growing orchids which will not tolerate a hot climate. Further, within a zone there may be micro climates influenced by such things as the proximity of the ocean or altitude. Most gardeners would have a feeling for the climate of the locality they live in and how it may differ from surrounding areas.

Orchid growers tend to be inveterate experimenters. Many succeed in growing good plants in environments somewhat less than the ideal. If your minimum temperatures are marginally less than those recommended in this book, trial and error may enable you to create an environment where some hybrids or particular cultivars will still be rewarding to grow.

Hints For Beginners

Buying plants. Resist buying large plants not in flower, unless a well-known variety, as the flowers may be disappointing to you. Avoid buying large plants that don't seem ever to have flowered. If the previous owner could not flower it you probably won't be able to either.

Watering. Many beginners kill more plants by watering too often than for any other reason. Even experienced growers find it difficult to resist the urge to do it. When in doubt, don't water.

Pests. Some insects are friendly but it is best to treat any unidentified insect among your orchids as an enemy.

Fertilizer. Do not be too heavy-handed with plant nutrients. Better too little than too much.

Large pots. Resist the urge to put an orchid in too large a pot where it will sulk. In general orchids are grown in pots of a smaller size than you would find ordinary pot plants of the same size.

Visit other growers. Just seeing how others grow their plants is a tremendous help.

Orchid societies. If there is one in your area you will find they offer help for beginners. It will open doors for you to visit other growers.

The internet. If you have a computer, the internet is a source of a massive amount of information about orchids. There are many lists and chat sites you can subscribe to (usually free) where experts, often several, will answer any orchid problems or queries you post.

Plants for beginners. Not everybody will agree with this short list but try any of the following to start with:

Laelia anceps	*Cymbidium* hybrids
Coelogyne cristata	*Epidendrum radicans*
Dendrobium kingianum	*Epidendrum ibaguense*
Paphiopedilum insigne	*Oncidium flexuosum*

Persevere. Do not get discouraged if some of your first plants do not do well or even die. Many very successful growers will tell you they have been through this phase. Persevere and you may be surprised how quickly and suddenly you can gain an intuitive insight into the needs of these plants.

CHAPTER 1

History

Exotic orchids, although few in variety and numbers, were being cultivated in England by the end of the 18th century. The plants were to be found mainly in a few botanical gardens. But this was to change.

Interest in the culture of orchids seems to have been first aroused in the early 19th century. A number of things probably contributed to this, but much of the credit is often given to a Mr. William Cattley who grew some new plant material included with other tropical plants sent to him from South America. One of the plants flowered in 1818 and created something of a sensation. It was shown to botanist John Lindley (who is still regarded as one of the most important orchid taxonomists of all time) and Lindley named the plant *Cattleya labiata*. This was in honor of Cattley and in appreciation of the beautiful lip of the flower. It seems, however, that Swainson, the man who collected Cattley's plants in Brazil, disappeared before he got around to telling anyone exactly where he found them. It was over 70 years before *Cattleya labiata* was rediscovered.

In Cattley's day it was fashionable for the landed gentry and otherwise affluent people to have large greenhouses on their estates. These were heated to tropical temperatures by steam pipes from a boiler fired with coal. A servant had to rise from his bed every night to keep the fire stoked. They called these structures stove-houses and in them a variety of tropical plants flourished. Into them were placed orchid plants sent to England by plant collectors. There, a few orchids used to the conditions presumably survived, but most languished and eventually died. Slowly, as more information about

Opposite: *Phragmipedium longifolium*

how and where orchids grew in nature filtered through from plant collectors, orchids were taken out of stove conditions, given more light, more air, less heat and suitable growing media. They grew and flowered and interest in acquiring and growing them accelerated.

The days of the plant hunters had arrived. Some were sent out by wealthy patrons. Most were hired by several large nurseries that, as there seemed to be money to be made by trading in orchids, specialized in them. Some of the large and more famous of these in England included James Veitch & Son, Stuart Low and Frederick Sander. The last is said to have had 20 collectors in the field at one time. Orchids were stripped from forests and sent to Europe, thousands of plants often in one consignment. Losses during a long sea voyage were often horrific, entire consignments frequently arriving dead. By early Victorian times orchids had become something of a status symbol with the wealthy. Plants of any special merit or rareness changed hands at what today would be regarded as astronomical prices.

In nature, orchids grow in symbiosis with a fungus. This relationship is called a **mycorrhiza**. Again in nature, orchid seed will not germinate without being infected by the fungus, a frustrating situation for early growers who could not find any way of easily propagating orchids from seed. This was particularly so as an orchid seed capsule may contain anything up to a million or more dust-like seeds. The minute seeds possess only a small sphere of undifferentiated tissue and no food reserves at all.

About the beginning of the 20th century the work of European scientists Bernard and Burgeff, working independently, resulted in the successful

Lycaste Koolena 'June'

needed by plants plus sucrose – ordinary table sugar. When Knudsen's work was originally published, some critics proclaimed that it was well-established that orchids grew only in symbiosis with fungus and that plants raised in a sterile environment could not possibly survive to flowering size. Knudsen confounded the critics by growing a cattleya hybrid to adult size entirely in sterile containers and presenting the plant in flower.

Although his original formula has been improved, most new orchids are raised by Knudsen's methods. Young plants so raised are, until they flower, called seedlings.

In humans, the children of the same parents will not all look exactly the same unless they are identical twins – this happens with orchids too. To the early growers any orchid one could get hold of was worth cultivating. Hybridization has vastly improved both the floral quality and availability of present-day plants. Even so, the very best plant from a large batch of seedlings often changed hands at a relatively large price and most of us could only admire these from pictures in books. But the price of superior plants fell dramatically after the 1960s when techniques were developed to enable most kinds of orchids to be tissue-cultured. These plants are termed **mericlones**, the first syllable being derived from the meristematic tissue taken to initiate the process and the second indicating that the plant is in effect a propagation of the mother plant. The price of mericlones is usually only a little higher than seedlings, so we can all own pieces of many of the top orchids. Unfortunately plants are sometimes distributed which do not grow properly or have other problems.

Orchid growers did not escape the deprivations and tragedies suffered by the rest of the population during the two world wars. Difficulty in obtaining supplies of fuel to heat the greenhouse was a major problem. At the beginning of World War II some commercial growers in England sent plants overseas to save them. Large consignments of unflowered cymbidium seedlings sent to Australia created an interest in this genus with a large post-

germination of orchid seeds in an otherwise sterile medium in which a culture of the right fungus had been established. Unfortunately this did not result in a flood of cheap orchid seedlings becoming available as most commercial nurserymen found the process too technical and difficult. An exception was Joseph Charlesworth, a man with no scientific training, who mastered the process and by 1909 was hybridizing and raising odontoglossum seedlings by the thousands at his nursery at Haywards Heath in Sussex. Most crispum type hybrids around today trace their ancestry back to Charlesworth's stud plants.

In 1922 came a breakthrough which saw the prices of orchid plants plummet. One no longer had to be wealthy to grow orchids as a hobby. The breakthrough was made by Professor Knudsen of Cornell University who pointed out that the mycorrhiza made carbohydrates in the form of simple sugars available to the plant. He successfully germinated and grew orchids *in vitro* in a sterile medium comprising all the inorganic elements

Sarcochilis Melba

war increase in the number of commercial establishments and hobbyists growing the plants. With the emergence, post-war, of reliable international air services, Australia pioneered a cut-flower industry air freighting cymbidium blooms to the Northern Hemisphere in their off-season.

Our vanishing rainforests are an ecological disaster of a magnitude not seen on our planet in historical times. Thousands of acres are being destroyed every day. Some orchid species are endemic in only a small area, and with the destruction of its environment, that species becomes extinct in the wild. Over-collection of plants in some areas still occurs, but nothing on the scale of what was done in the 19th century. An international convention, CITES (Convention on International Trade in Endangered Species), seeks to closely control the collecting and exporting of endangered species and all orchids, whether endangered or not, are on the CITES Schedule. The problem with CITES is that it may be allowing more orchids to be destroyed than it is saving.

Many orchid growers would welcome the opportunity of saving orchids from destruction in doomed forests. But if you decided to travel to such an area to collect and take home plants from trees felled for timber or agriculture, CITES, or the local legislation enacted to give effect to it, could be enforced by the local bureaucracy in a way that would prohibit any attempts to save the plants. Or, at best, it would place as many obstacles in the way of your obtaining the various necessary permits as it would if you were taking plants from living forests. So a new threat to orchid conservation in nature has emerged – legislation.

On a more hopeful note an increasing number of species, whose natural habitats have been destroyed, are now being preserved in the collections of orchid growers. And still on a hopeful note there is evidence of an increasing body of world opinion in favor of making CITES more conservation-orientated and perhaps a little less trade-orientated where the two are in conflict.

CHAPTER 2

Some Basics

Orchids are not difficult to grow. It is believed by many that orchids are mysterious and expensive plants – to be grown only in costly, steamy greenhouses by people with very specialized knowledge. In short, not plants for the ordinary gardener to contemplate growing. None of this is true.

There are, however, important basic cultural differences between orchids and most other garden plants. Many orchids grow on trees and their roots dry out between rain showers. You would have to try hard to kill one of these orchids by withholding water – and it would take a long time. And most orchids are not grown in soil but in an inert medium which dries out quickly. They would die if planted in soil alongside your cabbages. The cabbages, on the other hand, would die even more quickly if they were put into orchid medium and their roots allowed to dry out. Understand these two differences and you already have the basics of successful orchid culture. There are no other mysteries.

Of course, as with garden plants, many orchids have individual preferences of different kinds. For example, some orchids do not like intense sunlight and need some degree of shading. If you are growing tropical kinds and live in a colder climate the orchids will need shelter from the elements.

Cymbidiums are popular on the West Coast of the United States as they can be grown in containers in the garden or in shade-houses but perhaps brought into shelter when flowering. In Florida, the very popular cattleya alliance can be grown on or in containers hung from suitable trees,

Opposite: *Doritaenopsis* Hinacity Glow 'Wanchyan'

but standard cymbidiums are difficult to bring into flower there, at least outdoors. Many orchids can be grown indoors near a window, and so can be enjoyed in whatever climate you live in.

Acquiring plants

Advice often given to a beginner is to provide twice the growing area originally intended and then to buy half the number of plants. Many of us have experienced the frustration of having a growing area·so full of plants there is just no room left to put those special orchids one wants to purchase. A beginner is advised to acquire only plants that suit the conditions under which he or she is able to grow them. Be cautious about purchasing adult plants that have flowered but are not in flower at the time. If the vendor is culling plants with inferior flowers they should be priced accordingly.

Unflowered seedlings are usually available in great variety and are a good way of building a collection of plants quickly. The price will depend upon the quality and reputation of the parent plants and how far off the seedlings are from reaching flowering size. The cheapest way to buy plants is likely to be in flasks of unflowered seedlings. However, depending upon your conditions and growing skills, these can take from three to five years or more to reach flowering size. Some of the seedlings from a flask will grow faster than others. Mericlones can be more expensive but enable the acquisition of some of the best orchids of superior quality. If purchasing small plants, ask to be satisfied that they are not "runts" which have been out of the flasks for some years and will not grow satisfactorily.

Dendrobium kingianum group showing color range.

Temperature

Many of the warm orchids can still be grown successfully in colder climates but must be grown indoors where the temperature can be controlled. This can be in the home or in a greenhouse. In both cases the warm air needs to be circulated with a fan and controlled by a thermostat. Where available, natural gas is popular for greenhouses, and it is cheaper than electricity. Natural gas heaters must be vented to the outside as the fumes are likely to be harmful to the orchids. A portable gas heater with a pressurized tank is useful in a cold climate in an emergency – even unvented this is better than freezing the plants.

It is often more difficult to cool plants than it is to heat them. In the home, this may be as simple as moving the plant away from heat sources and sunlight. In greenhouses, it is more complicated. The only practical method is evaporative cooling. The deluxe system uses a fogger. This produces a literal fog of water that mostly evaporates before it hits the plants. To evaporate, the water droplets must extract energy from the air, thereby cooling it. A cheaper method is to install jets that are available for the purpose and will produce a fine mist from household water pressures. These work quite well if placed in front of ventilators through which air is entering the greenhouse. The lower the relative humidity (i.e. the drier the air) entering, the greater the cooling effect and vice versa.

Temperature is measured by a thermometer placed in the shade where sunlight will not fall on it to give a misleading reading. Indispensable for both the home and greenhouse is a maxi-mini thermometer that records the highest and lowest temperatures experienced between re-settings. It tells you what has been happening to temperatures during your absence. Actually, maximum leaf temperatures are more important to the orchid than air temperatures. You will not have an instrument to read these, but if the leaf feels cool all is well. If the leaf is quite hot to the touch, the plant will be under stress. The leaves are heated mostly by radiant energy from the sun. If all else fails, shade the plants more, even if this means they receive a lot less light than they should.

Many orchids need a seasonal drop in temperature at night to initiate flowers. If the difference between day and night temperatures is not great enough during the critical period, they will not flower. There are growers who cultivate orchids with night temperatures regularly dropping below those recommended, but some genera are more tolerant of this than others. An occasional drop in temperature below that recommended will not harm most kinds. Do watch for very low or high temperatures immediately adjacent to glass windows. Even where seasonal temperature minimums are not essential to initiate flowering, orchids usually need a day-night differential for best growth. In a greenhouse, shade-house or in the garden this will not be a problem as temperatures naturally fall during the hours of darkness. However, in the home, room thermostats should be adjusted or other means employed to provide a temperature drop of at least 10 percent or preferably more, for most of the night.

Light

Some orchids grow naturally in the open under full sunlight but may require a little shading when brought into cultivation. Epiphytes growing in trees will get filtered light but those growing under a particularly dense forest canopy or on the forest floor are definitely low-light orchids.

Light intensity in popular orchid literature is expressed in foot-candles. The metric measurement is the lux. Light intensity in summer months can be over 10,000 foot-candles. Multiply foot-candles by 10.8 to get lux. Orchids in cultivation are typically grown under light levels of 1500-5000 foot-candles. The light requirements of various kinds of orchids are discussed further in the later chapters relating to them.

A very rough guide to light intensity is to observe the shadow cast by a hand held at about 12 in (30 cm) above a leaf. If the shadow has sharply defined edges light intensity will not be less than 5000 foot-candles. If the edges are not sharp but the outline of a hand can be seen this indicates about 3000 foot-candles. If a

Dendrobium French Lace. *Den. falcorostrum* was one parent.

shadow is cast, but what is making it is not obvious, light is probably under 2000 foot-candles. Shade-cloth for covering shade-houses is marketed under a figure indicating the amount of shade provided. Thus 25 percent shade-cloth lets through 75 percent of the sunlight. This measurement is presumably with the sun at right angles to the cloth. If the sun is coming in obliquely less light will come through.

Leaf color can indicate light intensity, with darker green suggesting less light. However, normal leaf color will vary with different kinds of orchids. If in doubt, it is better to give more light than less. If the plants are flowering regularly in due season they will be receiving enough light. A camera with a light meter can be used to give an indication of light levels. Set the camera for an ASA film rating of between 100 and 120 and the shutter speed at 1/250 second. Place a large white reflective surface (e.g. a sheet of plain paper) at right angles to the sun.

Dendrobium Doreen, a phalaenopsis-type dendrobium.

Position the camera so the white surface fills the view finder. The correct lens aperture for the above settings will give a rough measurement as follows:

f 4	250 foot-candles
f 5.6	500 foot-candles
f 8	1000 foot-candles
f 11	2000 foot-candles
f 16	4000 foot-candles

Air movement and humidity

If the air is holding all the water, in the form of water vapor, that it is capable of at that temperature, it is said to be saturated. The relative humidity is said to be 100 percent. If the air is holding only half the amount of water vapor it is capable of holding at that temperature, the relative humidity is 50 percent and so on. Orchids prefer a relative humidity in excess of 50 percent. If it falls too much below 40 percent on a hot day the plants can be under stress. They particularly resent strong drafts of hot, dry air. If air movement is used to cool leaves on hot days, then the higher the humidity the better.

Providing a reasonably humid environment can be difficult in the home. Air-conditioning systems, heaters, even soft furnishing, which absorb moisture, all conspire to lower air humidity indoors. However, a humid environment is not always ideal for the other occupants. Humidity can be raised by placing plants together, misting the plants, putting them near a humidifier, or sitting the plants on a gravel tray, where water is added until it almost covers the stones.

As heat from the sun raises greenhouse temperatures, the relative humidity will fall unless additional water is taken up. The foggers and water jets discussed previously will not only provide evaporative cooling but will also get more water into the air. These can be further assisted by damping down all the paths and walls in the greenhouse and even misting the plants if they will dry out before nightfall.

It is useful to have a means of measuring the relative humidity and there are two options. A wet bulb thermometer is really two in one with the bulb of one kept wet. The readings from the two will be different and when related to a chart will give an accurate humidity reading. More popular is a different device with a direct reading dial showing the relative humidity at a glance. The latter may not be very accurate, but gives a useful enough indication.

Humidity can be counterproductive at night-time as the temperature falls. The air reaches saturation point and must somehow get rid of some of the water it is holding. The colder areas, such as plastic or glass, are the first to get wet. However, if a dew is on the plants, they will be at a greater risk from disease. Raising the air temperature inside marginally over the outside air temperature can prevent this. Moving air over the plants is also beneficial.

CHAPTER 3

Nomenclature

Species and hybrids

The name of an orchid and the way that name is written can give you a wealth of information about that plant. For example, if it is a hybrid the name alone will enable you to trace its ancestry back to species and even tell you who made and named the plant.

If the plant is a **species**, the name is always written down in italics in a binominal system. Thus in *Laelia flava* the second word is the species name and *Laelia* is the **genus** name – the name given to the group of species to which *Laelia flava* belongs. The genus name always begins with a capital letter. If a **hybrid** is made between *Laelia flava* and, say, *Sophronitis coccinea* it has been given a name, *Sophrolaelia* Marriottiana. You know that Marriottiana is a cultivated hybrid and not a species because it is not written in italics. It is called the **grex** or collective name. If we cross this hybrid with, say, a *Cattleya* the new **intergeneric hybrid** name is a *Sophrolaeliocattleya*. If we make a further hybrid and introduce yet a fourth genus it becomes more difficult to coin an intergeneric name that gives you a useful idea of what genera were involved. A list of some of the intergeneric hybrid names is in the back of this book.

Abbreviations

A feature of the orchid family is that so many hybrids have been cultivated, whereas in nature, natural hybrids between species are not common and intergeneric hybrids very uncommon. To simplify the writing down of genera and intergeneric hybrids they can be abbreviated. Thus *L.* for *Laelia*, *C.* for *Cattleya*, *Soph.* for *Sophronitis*, *Slc.* for *Sophrolaeliocattleya* and so on.

Sophrolaeliocattleya Madge Fordyce 'Red Orb'

Cultivar names

Sophrolaelia Marriottiana was first flowered in 1896, but although this hybrid has been remade several times since then, the name remains the same. As most of the progeny of the two parents will look in some degree different from their siblings, an individual can be given a further name, called a **cultivar** name. Thus, although there are many plants of *Sl.* Marriottiana around there is only one *Sl.* Marriottiana 'Flares'.

The cultivar name can be recognized because it follows the others and is always enclosed in single quotation marks. Only plants of outstanding quality are given cultivar names. It may be helpful to think of the hybrid name (grex name) as the family name and the cultivar names as the names of the children of that family.

Sander's List

With over 100,000 grex names in existence does anybody attempt to keep track of them all? The answer is that they do, and we are indebted to Mr. Frederick Sander who, at about the end of the 19th century, commenced to note and publish the names of all the new hybrids that were being made. Sander's list of orchid hybrids was maintained by the Sander family until 1946, when the work and publication of it was taken over by the Royal Horticultural Society (RHS). It now runs to no fewer than 10 volumes.

With Sander's lists one can ascertain whether a hybrid has been made between any two hybrids or species and what name has been given to it. It can tell you what the parents of any hybrid were. You can construct a family tree of the hybrid. If the hybrid goes back many generations to the species in its ancestry this will take quite a long time if one has to search through 10 volumes. Happily, with a computer there is now an alternative which is much cheaper (a set of Sander's is not cheap) and will do the family tree for you in seconds. The complete work has been digitized and is available on a single disk. There are two programs on the market:

RHS CD-ROM. This contains all the Sander's hybrid data plus details of awards granted by five orchid societies, with pictures of some of these flowers. Also other relevant material.

Catasetum tenebrosum – the female flower. But is it beautiful?

WILDCATT ORCHIDS database. This has all the Sander's hybrid data plus details of awards granted by two orchid societies. There are no pictures, but these disks are updated more frequently. This may be the more popular program.

Hybrid registration

To be legitimate, the name of a new hybrid (i.e. the grex name) has to be registered with the International Registration Authority for Orchid Hybrids in England. If you have raised a new hybrid, an application for registration is likely to be accepted if

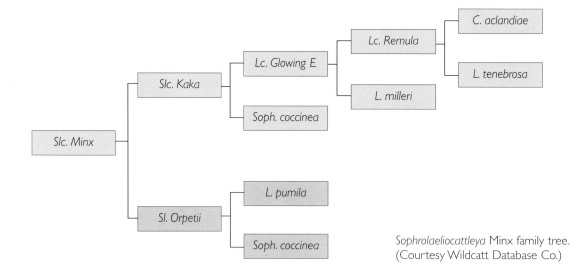

Sophrolaeliocattleya Minx family tree. (Courtesy Wildcatt Database Co.)

the Registrar is satisfied that you hybridized, raised and flowered the cross (or have the permission of the one who did), that the two parents involved have not been crossed and named before by someone else and that the name you have chosen is acceptable. The chosen name must not have been used previously for some other hybrid in the same general orchid alliance. If the application for registration is approved, details will be published and will appear in Sander's in due course with credit to you as the originator.

Cultivar names

Anyone can, in theory, give an orchid a cultivar name. There is no general system for registering or recording cultivar names. Despite this, instances of the same plant appearing at various times and places with a different name are not common. This is due in part to the fact that the emergence of a cultivar of exceptional quality is usually given wide publicity in orchid literature. To be legitimate, a cultivar name is supposed to be published somewhere. Cultivar names must be fancy names not in Latin form.

Name changes

Taxonomists frequently change the names of plant species. They may decide that a species has been assigned to the wrong genus or they may create new genera for species that they believe do not fit in where they were first assigned. Or, again, perhaps research shows that a species was given a name in error at the outset and that some other name has priority. We often resent having to change the labels on plants. On a different note, imagine you discovered that one of your very early ancestors who lived 150 years ago had a different surname from what you understood. The family tree you had constructed going back this far could be thrown into chaos. Sander's lists wisely ignore name changes in species. Thus, because *Cyrtochilum macranthum* was once known as *Oncidium macranthum*, it appears as such in Sander's lists.

Masdevallia tovarensis 'Snow White'

Alternative names

In this book, species are referred to under the names believed to be currently accepted for them. Where a species is known, or has recently been known, under another name, this name follows written in brackets. We are of course talking only about species. Under the hybrid registration system, orchids have a recorded genealogy not equaled in any other plant family and changes in hybrid names are very rarely necessary.

Awards

Many orchid societies give quality awards to new orchids of outstanding quality. For example the American Orchid Society (AOS) can grant three quality awards. These are, in descending order of merit, FCC (First Class Certificate), AM (Award of Merit) and HCC (Highly Commended Certificate). The award is usually appended when the plant name is written down. Thus *Cym.* Pink Passion 'Cloudnine' HCC/AOS. Some societies use other terms such as Gold, Silver and Bronze awards.

CHAPTER 4

The Growing Environment

Orchids in the home

You do not have to have a greenhouse to grow orchids. If you can grow a houseplant, you can enjoy growing orchids. Also, if your climate is suitable, orchids grown indoors over winter can be moved outside to a protected area for the summer.

As light is essential for orchids, the plants will need to be close to an east or west window, or a lightly shaded south-facing window. Orchids have been

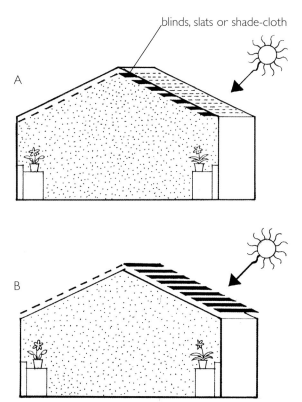

In both cases plants receive the same shade, but B, with blinds or shade-cloth outside, runs cooler because only the wanted light is allowed to generate heat.

grown successfully under these conditions, but avoid those requiring very high light levels. On a window facing more to the east or west *Phalaenopsis* will grow well if the room temperature does not fall too low in cold weather. Other low-light orchids which will flower with this orientation include, to mention a few, *Phragmipedium*, *Paphiopedilum*, *Miltoniopsis* and, in some locations, some of the more temperature-tolerant *Masdevallia*.

It may be helpful in difficult situations to supplement what natural light there is with artificial light. This topic is the subject of Chapter 9, Growing under Lights.

The shade-house

Whatever your local climate, orchids are going to need at least as much shading as they would have in their natural environment. A shade-house is usually a wooden or metal framework covered with a monofilament black shade-cloth. The pitch needs to be reasonably steep or some support such as wire netting placed under the shade-cloth to prevent it from sagging. Before we had plastic shade-cloth these structures were usually constructed with wooden laths to control the light. Lath houses are still being erected and provide very solid, low-maintenance housing.

It is common practice to cover the shade-house with a transparent plastic cover to protect flowers during the flowering season. The better modern plastics contain an ultraviolet inhibitor (that stops UV destroying plastic) and are quite long-lasting. A totally enclosed shade-house should not only give control over light but also give protection against insects, winds and, where needed, light frosts. A house with a permanent roof to keep rain out, but open at the sides, is a popular structure for year-

Light is essential when growing orchids indoors and so they should be placed near an east or west window, or a lightly shaded south-facing window.

round cultivation of cooler-growing orchids, such as cymbidiums, where protection from only light frosts is necessary. This arrangement is common even in tropical countries, where similar protection from rain is required.

The greenhouse

A greenhouse is usually thought of as an enclosed structure where the grower can attempt to create a climate similar to that experienced by the plants in their natural environment. Temperature, light, humidity and air movement were discussed briefly earlier. The control of light intensity does present practical problems. When greenhouses were glass-houses it was relatively easy to paint shading material on the glass in summer and remove most of it during the winter. Various kinds of plastics have largely replaced glass. They have the advantage of

needing a less exacting framework and of providing a more watertight long-term covering. Some modern materials seem to be long-lasting – but just how long

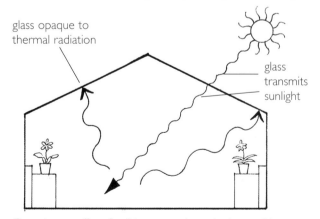

Greenhouse effect. Sunlight passes through glass and heats the interior, generating long-wave thermal (heat) radiation that is absorbed by the glass, trapping much of the sun's energy within.

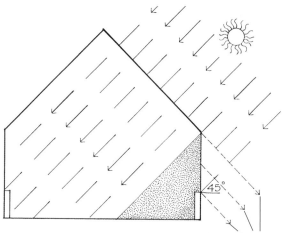

Sunlight Reflection. When the angle shown is much greater than 45°, most of the sunlight is reflected and plants near this wall will be in relative shade. Turn this to your advantage when positioning plants with differing light requirements.

Malaxis autocentrum on a tree in Papua New Guinea rainforest.

remains to be seen. You can't paint shading materials on most of them. The alternative is shade-cloth. If fixed on the outside, the inside temperature will run cooler because unwanted light is not allowed to enter and contribute to interior heating. If on the inside, the same degree of shading is provided but the unwanted light also raises temperatures. Shade-cloth is usually fixed inside the greenhouse because, despite the disadvantages, it is less of a nuisance to control there.

A wide choice of aluminium-framed greenhouses supplied in kit form for do-it-yourself assembly is currently available. A spanner and a screwdriver are almost the only tools needed to erect them. Most have clear plastic down to ground level and, although we do not grow orchids down there, light entering under the benches adds to the internal heat in hot weather and to heat loss in cold weather. Small greenhouses suffer from greater temperature extremes than larger ones. Ideal is a greenhouse erected on a wall of poured concrete, cement blocks or bricks to bench height. Otherwise the external walls under the benches can have the light obscured and/or insulating material secured over them. Benches should be about 30 in (76 cm) high – much lower for large plants such as cymbidiums.

Free-standing greenhouses usually have a pitched roof or gable roof. There have been arguments for over 100 years as to whether these are best oriented north/south or east/west. East/west will allow much more winter light through the roof at lower latitudes but may run hotter in summer.

Very often there is little choice of either location or orientation on a small section of land – the greenhouse has to be sited where it will conveniently go. Shading by buildings or trees is undesirable. Lean-to structures built against a solid wall or the side of a building can give quite good results. They should be against a more or less south-facing wall to get good day length. If your home has a sunroom getting good daylight hours you probably already have a "greenhouse", which can be shared by people and plants.

CHAPTER 5

Growing Media and Containers

Orchids have been said to grow in almost any-thing. Not quite true, but from time to time excellent orchids have been exhibited with their roots in the most unlikely composts – i.e. growing media. A grower once produced fine-looking orchids in horse manure!

Experienced orchid growers tend to be inveterate experimenters and this is to be encouraged, as it has led to many improved cultural practices. The novice, however, is best advised to keep to conventional recipes for growing media.

Above: *Ceratocentron fesselii* 'Sparkles', a miniature from the Philippines.

The ideal potting medium should encourage rather than inhibit root growth, should not be toxic to the plant and should be very slow to decompose. Above all, it should give the roots plenty of air and must dry out quickly if used for epiphytes or lithophytes. The roots of these orchids, in nature, may dry out daily and will not survive in continually wet material. To achieve both these requirements the potting medium must have a high air capacity. This is the percentage of the total volume of the material which is air. It should be 30 percent or more for epiphytes. A medium entirely composed of very fine organic material will have a low air capacity, will starve the roots of oxygen and remain wet for a long time, leading to root rot.

Materials used

Materials which have been incorporated in potting mixes include pine bark, perlite, pumice, scoria or lava rock, coarse sand or gravel, sphagnum moss, rock wool, peat, coconut fiber, expanded polystyrene, vermiculite, cork and fern fiber. The last is not the osmunda fiber used years ago and not now available but the coarse fibers from various tree ferns available in some countries. Pine bark alone is successfully used by many growers to cultivate a wide range of genera. A good all-around particle size is $^1/_5$ in (5 mm) to $^2/_5$ in (10 mm), but finer and coarser grades than this are marketed. If one is a perfectionist, the fine grades could be selected for use in small pots which can otherwise dry out too quickly and the coarse grades for plants in large pots. The bark grade mentioned above has an air capacity of about 50 percent when used by itself.

Douglas fir (*Pseudotsuga menziesii*), red fir (*Abies magnifica*), white fir (*Abies concolor*), Monterey pine (*Pinus radiata*) and redwood (*Sequoia* species) are some of the pines that provide orchid bark. Orchids, like rhododendrons, prefer to have their roots in something a shade more acidic than most other plants.

Pine bark, however, is usually a little too acidic and benefits from the addition of up to $^1/_2$ oz of lime to a two-gallon bucket of bark – about 2 g to 1 liter. If in doubt, use a smaller amount of lime. Dolomite lime, a mixture of calcium carbonate and magnesium carbonate, is preferable as it provides a long-term supply of magnesium and calcium for the orchid. Sprinkling a little lime on the surface after the orchid is potted might be an alternative treatment but do not overdo it.

Bark of any grade should come with the fine grades screened out of it. This is not essential, but at least the very fine particles and dust must be removed even if you have to do it yourself by putting it through a fine-mesh screen. A less labor-intensive method for large quantities is to leave the bark in a tank of water for a week or two. If it is then carefully removed from the top, the particles and dust will remain as a sludge on the bottom. Fresh from the tree, the bark contains

volatile material that is suspected of inhibiting plant growth for a period. The water treatment just mentioned will help, but the ideal is to spread the bark out and expose it to rain and sun. Do not have it in contact with soil, as it could pick up diseases. Some vendors condition their product for immediate use before putting it on the market.

Countless recipes for media have been published over the years, many tried and many discarded. A safe one to use with epiphytes such as cattleyas is:

Medium grade bark	8
Pumice	2
Total parts by volume	10

One of the other inorganic materials mentioned can be substituted for pumice. The particle size should not be larger than the bark and preferably smaller. A heavier mix suitable for cymbidiums is:

Pumice	4
Fine bark	2
Peat	4
Total parts by volume	10

Laelia lucasiana × *Cattleya walkeriana*

The peat should be a suitable kind – preferably sphagnum moss peat. Peat is acidic and before incorporation must have dolomite lime added at double the rate suggested for bark.

Sphagnum moss, alive or not (but not decayed), is commonly used by orchid growers. It is useful for promoting new root growth on plants with decayed roots. Shredded, it is incorporated in many mixes. And although it seems to break all the rules, there are growers who succeed in cultivating some genera in moss alone. In this case a layer of inert material is usually placed on top to suppress growth of algae. A suitable grade of moss such as New Zealand sphagnum moss is essential. The orchids suited to sphagnum moss culture are mentioned in later chapters devoted to specific requirements for different genera.

Pots

Unglazed clay or earthenware pots are excellent plant containers. The roots like to adhere to the surface and the medium tends to dry out more quickly and more evenly than in plastic pots, which tend to dry out from the top surface first. Nevertheless, plastic pots have largely replaced clay pots for orchid culture. Select black pots which last longer and attract the heat. Plastic pots may be re-used if they are first sterilized to prevent possible transfer of disease. They should be thoroughly washed with detergent and then soaked for at least two hours in a strong solution of bleach, i.e. calcium hypochlorite or sodium hypochlorite. Clay pots can be given similar treatment, but really need to be also put in an oven and subjected to at least one hour of dry heat at 300°F (150°C).

Baskets

Baskets (called rafts if they are square), usually constructed of strips of wood leaving most of the sides open, suit some orchids. Suitable but less favored are wire baskets.

The genus *Stanhopea*, for instance, sends flower stems downwards and these emerge from the bottom or sides of the basket. In a pot, these flower stems have nowhere to go.

Monopodials, such as vandas, have roots that like to wander around in the air. They resent being confined to pots and are suitable for basket culture.

Gomesa crispa, illustrating raft culture.

Fine potting material is obviously unsuitable for a basket but large chunks of pine bark, charcoal or tree fern are used successfully.

Slabs

Orchids can be mounted on slabs of tree fern fiber or on the outer surface of virgin cork. Some genera, such as *Tolumnia*, just have to get their roots dry even more rapidly than most epiphytes after watering. For this reason, they are widely grown on slabs. Other suitable subjects include those smaller orchids that have long rhizomes, make multiple leads and are a nuisance to keep in pots because they quickly grow over the side.

Slabs are suspended vertically with the plant mounted on the side and facing the sun. They need watering frequently, ideally more than once a day in hot, dry conditions. A small section cut from the branch of a tree can be used for slab culture but not any tree will do. Observe what other orchid growers in your area are using successfully. Otherwise select a branch from a tree that supports a growth of moss or lichen. The branch is split lengthwise and the plant mounted on the bark side.

No matter what kind of slab is used, the plant must be secured firmly to it to get it established. With the tree branch or cork, galvanized steel staples driven over the rhizome do a good job. Otherwise tie it on with wire – not plastic material that will stretch in time. The wire can be removed only when there is sufficient root growth along and through the slab to secure the plant.

Some plants like to extend new growths upwards and a few insist on growing downwards. They should be positioned accordingly. Most are simply mounted in the middle. When a plant covers the slab, fix it to a larger one. A new idea is to construct a "virtual slab" from a length of plastic netting. Roll the netting into a cylinder, fasten it with wire and fill it with bark or other potting material. Attach the plant to the outside of the cylinder.

Saccolabium quisumbingi growing on a cork slab.

CHAPTER 6

Watering and Feeding

Orchid growers tend to worry too much about the quality of their water supply. Orchids are supposed to do best if the water is slightly on the acidic side, with a pH of about 6.5. However, they have been grown successfully in alkaline water with a pH of 7.5. Most municipal water supplies will present no problems, but there are exceptions. Water high in calcium and magnesium salts can be very hard and not lather easily so the householder often puts it through a water softener. This replaces calcium and magnesium with sodium. Sodium in large quantities is bad news for orchids, which will prefer the untreated water.

Above: Cirrhopetalum rothschildiana 'Red Chimney'

Some areas have water supplies very high in solutes (dissolved substances) that may have an effect on plant growth. The only useful way of improving this water in any quantity is to put it through a reverse osmosis device in which the water is put under pressure through a membrane. This results in two lots of water: one very low in solutes and the other very high in solutes that is then discarded. These setups are fairly expensive and waste a lot of water but many growers use them.

Rain water properly collected and stored is fine for orchids. Collection from an unpainted galvanized steel roof is unsuitable due to zinc toxicity. Painted metal roofs are probably safe, but if repainting such

Macroclinium bicolor

a roof ask the paint manufacturer to confirm their product is safe for drinking water. If so, it will be safe for orchids. Water collected from the various plastic coverings used on greenhouses should be safe. Rain water is best stored in a covered tank where it is protected from leaves and other wind-blown debris that could introduce disease organisms, particularly pythium and phytophthora. These diseases are spread to plants by infected water.

Watering practices

The growth of a plant can be limited by too little water but it is not a question of the frequency of irrigation. Orchids that must be dried out between waterings must always be dried out. But when it is time to water, do it well. The logistics of watering in both home and greenhouse needs to be thought out. When it is time to water, the potting mix needs to be thoroughly wet. This may mean taking the container to a sink, so the excess water can drain, or, if watering in place, removing excess water so the plant doesn't sit in water. The medium on the surface of the pot is not likely to show what conditions are like below. Push a finger down into it to get a better indication of whether the plant needs watering.

Epiphytes which need to dry out seem to make better growth with a short drying cycle and thus more frequent watering. If these plants remain regularly (not occasionally) wet for as long as a week there will be risk of root loss. The growing environment will need to be adjusted to correct this.

In the home, it can be difficult to adjust the watering regimen. The generally low humidity in the home causes the surface of the potting mix to dry out quickly, yet the generally lower light levels can mean the plant doesn't take up as much water as would be usual. The following are the main factors involved:

Remain wetter longer	Dry out quicker
Plastic pots	Clay pots
Large pots	Small pots
Low air capacity medium	High air capacity medium
High humidity	Low humidity
No air movement	Strong air movement
No or dormant roots	Many active roots
White pots	Black pots
Winter	Summer
Low temperatures	High temperatures
Low light	High light
Double-glazed greenhouse	No double-glazing
Twin-skinned greenhouse	Single-skinned greenhouse
Solid benches	Steel mesh benches

When using a hose in a greenhouse go back in half an hour and water the same pot again and repeat this even a third time. Labor-saving overhead sprinklers can be automated and are widely used by commercial growers. Most hobbyists, however, prefer to give plants individual attention.

Feeding

Attention to nutrition is essential to the cultivation of good orchids. Materials incorporated in the growing medium may contain some of the elements necessary for plant growth but they contribute little until the medium starts to break down. At this point it is usually discarded and the orchid repotted. Certain nutrients are sometimes incorporated in the medium when it is made up, but not those that dissolve on the first watering. The strength of the solution could then damage roots and be quickly washed right out. The modern practice is to put the nutrients in soluble form and much diluted in the water supply. Ideally this should be done every watering. Little and often is the key to successful nutrition.

NPK

A complete fertilizer mixture might have an NPK rating of, say, 20-20-20. These numbers describe the percentage of elemental nitrogen (N) and the oxides of phosphorus (P) and potassium (K).

The greatest need of a growing orchid is for nitrogen and 20-20-20 fertilizer is a good all-around one. Nitrogen requirements are highest when the plant is growing strongly under high light and lower during periods of dormancy or low light levels. Where there is difficulty in flowering, lowering the nitrogen intake often helps.

Other elements necessary for plant growth are calcium, magnesium and sulfur. Then there is a need, but in very minute quantities, for the so-called trace elements. These include boron, copper, manganese, molybdenum and zinc. Good, complete, soluble fertilizers sold for orchids should contain these in the correct proportions. Be cautious about adding them yourself as they can be toxic to the plant if applied in excess.

Calcium

Calcium deficiency is unusual but is occasionally reported in orchids. If lime was incorporated in the growing medium at the outset, calcium deficiency is probably unlikely. Municipal water supplies may contain some calcium, hard water a lot. Calcium is particularly mentioned here because commercial preparations seldom contain any at all. This is because it causes precipitates (deposits of solids) when added to concentrated liquid solutions as well as caking and other problems with dry mixes.

Calcium is a non-mobile element – the plant cannot move it from older parts of the plant to new growths if a deficiency occurs. For this reason, it ought to be available all the time. Calcium nitrate, if obtainable (it is widely used in commercial horticulture), can be added at the rate of about 0.02 oz per gallon or 150 milligrams per liter. If dissolved separately and added to the diluted feed solution there should be no precipitation. Use at double this strength if only applying occasionally.

Urea

Urea is the cheapest form of nitrogen and probably for this reason is often included in many soluble fertilizers on the market. Plant roots cannot take in urea. In soil it is broken down to compounds the roots can handle. In the kinds of inert media orchids are grown in, urea may break down in a way that releases nitrites and free ammonia, both of which are bad news for the roots. Urea is fine for foliar feeding. Not only can the leaves take it in safely, but urea may assist in the passage of other elements into the leaf. Most commercial preparations designed for foliar feeding are based on urea. Orchids can respond to foliar feeding but keep it very diluted and away from the roots.

Fertilizer strength

The NPK ratio itself does not tell you how much to use. The amount of each element in the liquid feed can be expressed in parts per million. Experiments have indicated that 100 ppm of nitrogen is about the optimum for most epiphytes and 150 ppm or more for heavy feeders such as cymbidiums. If about 0.07 oz of an NPK 20-20-20 fertilizer is dissolved in 1 gallon of water this will contain 100 ppm N, 44 ppm P and 83 ppm K. Very roughly, a level (not heaped) teaspoon is likely to be about 0.14 oz (4 g).

The strength of the feed should not be greatly exceeded any time you water. Putting 10 times the amount of fertilizer in the water every tenth watering

will do more harm than good. If using a proprietary brand of liquid fertilizer, it is a little more difficult unless you know how concentrated it is. When the product is specifically designed for orchids by a reputable company it is probably safe to follow the directions given. If in doubt, use it at half the recommended strength or less.

Slow-release fertilizers are available. The most popular with orchid growers are those that have inorganic salts released over a period of time through some kind of coating. These are a time-saver but there is little control over the rate of release or when the material is exhausted. Use them sparingly and keep them on top of the medium.

Sophrolaeliocattleya Trilogy 'Seminar'

CHAPTER 7

Pests and Diseases

Tales are told of herbivores such as cattle and deer munching orchids. A not-so-obvious culprit is the mouse. Mice are fond of flower buds and have been responsible for nibbling the ends off nearly all the buds in a small cymbidium collection, the owner

being at a loss to know what was causing the problem.

Insect pests

There are many large insects that can chew leaves and flowers. Spray with Orthene, Carbaryl or Diazinon.

Scale insects are sap-sucking pests and should be dealt with immediately any appear as they are difficult to eliminate if they get established in a collection. Spraying with Malathion or Diazinon will control them, but persistent treatment over a long period is required. Mineral oil sprays sold for use on green-leafed plants can be used, but follow the directions carefully. Swabbing with alcohol or methylated spirits gives immediate results. An effective home-made treatment is to use a mixture of a mild detergent, vegetable cooking oil and water in the ratio by volume of two parts detergent, 10 parts of oil to 1000 parts of water. Put the detergent and oil in a little water in a blender until it forms a white emulsion, then add the rest of the water. Adding Malathion or Diazinon at half full-strength will make the preparation even more effective. When spraying, be careful to cover not only the round female scales but also the dissimilar cotton-like male form.

Mealybugs are sluggish insects that appear white due to their surrounding cotton-like filaments. Like scale insects they are also sap-suckers and have a water-repellent exterior. They tend to hide in crevices and even in flowers. Any of the treatments suggested for scale should control them.

Aphids often build up in large numbers in buds, flowers and soft new growths before they are noticed. They are easy to kill with a wide range of

Scale. The white cotton-like masses are the male form.

insecticides including Diazinon, Malathion and Mavrik. Another option is Orthene which has both a contact and systemic action, being absorbed into the sap stream of the plant. Aphids are particularly unwelcome because they can harbor plant viruses.

Thrips are tiny fast-moving insects that rasp the surface of leaves and flowers and suck the sap. They leave silvery markings on leaves. Spray with any of the products suggested for aphids. Check the surface material of the potting mix as some species like to lurk there.

The two-spotted mite *Tetranychus urticae* is a bad pest of some orchids, including cymbidiums, where it will leave the underside of the leaves with a silvery appearance and a feel like sandpaper. The mite is straw-colored or reddish with the characteristic two black spots on the back. They proliferate in high temperatures and low humidity and dislike water. Two sprays 10 days apart with Kelthane (which does not kill the eggs) or Pentac are necessary. Do not use either of these materials more than three times running in 12 months as the two-spotted mite is notorious for evolving resistant strains. If necessary, switch to a spray in a different chemical group, such as Mavrik.

There are other mite species that will do damage, some small enough to need a magnifying glass to see them. If the sprays above are not effective on these, Malathion or Diazinon should be.

Slugs and snails need to be kept out of the growing area. Baits containing Mesurol or Metaldehyde will kill them. There is a tiny snail that hides in the pot where its presence is often not suspected until the plant is removed. The snail nibbles the ends and sides of the roots. Ordinary baits are not very effective. Destroy them physically after shaking the potting mix from the roots.

Chemicals mentioned above may be sold under different names viz:

Orthene (Acephate)	Malathion (Maldison)
Carbaryl (Sevin)	Mavrik (Taufluvalinate)
Diazinon (Knox Out)	Pentac (Dienochlor)

Fungi and bacteria

Prevention here is better than attempting to cure. That advice in itself is not very helpful unless you have some idea of the conditions favoring disease transmission.

Water is almost always involved in the establishment of these diseases. Some fungi release spores into the air and they may fall on healthy plants and infect them. The spores of the fungus *Botrytis* will germinate and infect when the relative humidity is near 100 percent, particularly if there is water (e.g. the merest film of dew) on the surface. This disease is the main one responsible for the spotting of flowers and it takes just six hours of favorable conditions for germination and infection to occur. Some diseases are spread by water infected at the source or splashing around from infected surfaces. These include bacterial rots and the soft black or brown rots caused by Pythium or Phytophthora. Do not allow stagnant water to remain in the crown or elsewhere on the plant.

There is a bewildering array of chemicals available to control diseases. Most are preventative; if the plant is coated with them the disease finds the environment too toxic to get established. Some

Dendrobium victoriae-reginae

fungicides are systemic, being able to enter, move around and protect the plant from within. Many modern fungicides are effective against some diseases but not against others and may even make them worse. The problem for the orchid grower is diagnosis and often hit-or-miss tactics have to be employed. The following shortlist is a sample of the chemicals available and the names under which they have been marketed.

Captan (Orthocide): a preventative fungicide effective against a wide range of fungal diseases. Can be used to drench potting media.

Mancozeb (Dithane, Manzate, Fore): another preventative fungicide effective against many diseases.

Rovral (Iprodione, Chipco): a preventative systemic fungicide with some eradicant action on established infections. Very effective against *Botrytis*. Unfortunately over-use will generate resistant strains of dis-

eases and this product should not be applied more than three times in 12 months.

Benlate (Benomyl): another systemic fungicide. Resistant strains quickly build up but being in a different chemical group it is useful to alternate with Rovral. Neither of these products should be regularly applied but they are reliable to have in reserve for emergencies. Neither is effective against Phytophthora or Pythium.

Aliette (fosetyl aluminum): a systemic absorbed by leaves and roots to give long-term protection against Phytophthora and Pythium. Has some curative effect.

Terrazole (Truban, Etridiazole): a soil drench effective against the same diseases as Aliette.

Quaternary ammonium compounds: trade names come and go for these, which are marketed for anything from eliminating moss and algae to treatment of swimming pools. They have been sold for plant protection under the names of Consan, Physan and RD20 among others. It is claimed they are effective against both bacterial and fungal diseases. Follow the directions, as they should be used greatly diluted. These are the only products among those mentioned above that will kill bacteria and they will often clean up small patches of wet rot on leaves if swabbed on or applied to diseased areas after the rotten tissue has been cut out. Useful, too, for controlling algae on walls and roofs.

Tactics

If a fungal or bacterial problem cannot be diagnosed, try everything until an effective solution is found. With soft brown or black rots try swabbing or flooding the infected area with Physan and drenching the roots with Aliette or Terrazole. If possible cut out the rot first. As a last resort try Rovral or Benlate, which treat some diseases with these symptoms. For leaf spotting try Rovral or Benlate once and then maintain regular spraying with a protective fungicide such as Captan or Mancozeb. Above all, try to correct the conditions that allowed the establishment of the disease, given that this may be easier said than done. Rotten roots may be hosting diseases but the prime cause is likely to be media remaining wet too long because it has broken down or has been watered too frequently. Tip the plant out of the pot and re-pot in a fresh pot with new medium after removing the decayed roots.

Viruses

Symptoms on the foliage include yellowish or dark streaks and blotches, or mottling, often with sunken leaf surfaces and occasionally in a diamond or mosaic pattern. Flowers may be streaked with brown, white or more intense colored markings. Diagnosis is often difficult as many of these symptoms can have origins other than a virus. If the same markings appear on every leaf or flower every year and other similar plants are "clean", a virus must be suspected. There is no cure and infected plants should be destroyed or isolated so they cannot infect others. A virus can be spread by insects but is more likely to be spread by the grower when handling plants, especially when re-potting or cutting off flowers. Wash hands between re-potting valuable plants and

Rhynchostylis coelestis

sterilize cutting tools by heating to a cherry red. Never use the same pot for another plant without sterilizing it first.

Weeds

Keep pots weed-free. Ferns that come up may look nice but they are competitors for the orchid and should be removed. A variety of *Oxalis corniculata* has become a worldwide pest of orchids. It fires shiny black seeds a considerable distance and the seedlings come up everywhere. They are easy to pull out when small but, when a large plant gets established next to a pseudobulb, removing the plant from the pot and shaking off all the potting medium can be necessary to remove it. This can be avoided by painting the weed with a solution of weedkiller. Glyphosate can be applied with a small artist's brush. Be very careful not to allow the weedkiller to contact any part of the orchid.

CHAPTER 8

Potting and Propagation

Preparing the pot

The drainage holes must be protected from becoming blocked – particularly important in a clay pot where there is usually only one hole. The most popular arrangement is to cover the bottom of the pots with large pieces of broken pots, polystyrene, stones or other similar material. These are termed crocks. They should be larger than the smallest drainage holes. Arrange the top of the crocks into a slope. This will enable gravity to drain the capillary water that would otherwise be held at the drainage interface between the crocks and the growing medium.

Do not put in more crocks just to reduce the volume of the growing medium. Better to put a small inverted pot at the bottom with pieces clipped out of the rim. This will have the benefit of providing an air space in the very area which is the last to dry out. Roots often rot in this area. Contrary to what may be thought, a test will show that extra crocks do not significantly shorten the time taken for water to drain through the pot if the drainage holes are not blocked.

Ascocenda Navy Blue

Re-potting

In a natural environment, the roots of a tree-dwelling epiphyte will grow around the outside of the tree trunk. In a pot, the roots are forced to grow against their nature – around and attached to the inside surface of the pot. It is difficult to remove a plant with healthy roots without damaging them but it cannot be helped. When the leading growth or growths are going to grow over the edge of the pot, the orchid must be removed and placed in a larger pot. Select one that will allow enough room for two

years' growth. But no more. Orchids can sulk if put in too large a pot.

The best time to re-pot is when new roots are just appearing from the base of the leading growth. Be very careful not to knock them off. A plant that has lost its roots because the potting medium has broken down and decayed should be re-potted at any time. If the roots are all healthy and in a solid clump, the root ball can be left undisturbed and new potting medium placed around it. Otherwise tease it apart and remove all rotten roots. Position the plant with

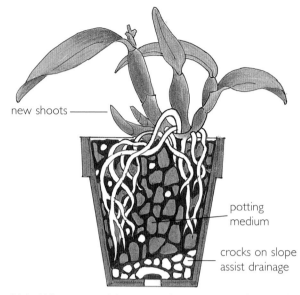

new shoots

potting medium

crocks on slope assist drainage

Right. Where to position roots when re-potting. Space left for new shoots to develop.

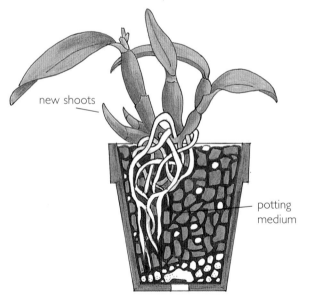

new shoots

potting medium

Wrong. Roots of re-potted plant forced into center of pot may rot. New shoots have no space to grow into.

the older portion against the side of the new pot, leaving space in front into which it can grow. The pot should always be oriented to keep this space facing the midday sun, i.e. facing the equator, as plants tend to grow in that direction. Support plants with few roots with a stake.

Dividing plants

When an orchid is already growing out of a large pot it may not be convenient or good culture to remove it to an even larger one. The alternative is to break the orchid into pieces. Do this by cutting the rhizome (the connecting stem between upright growths from which roots are produced) to make divisions of not less than three, and preferably four, pseudobulbs with leaves. The divisions with a leading (newest) growth should be potted as already described. The older back pieces will often make a new shoot if potted. With many kinds of orchids the surest way to get the most viable divisions is to cut the rhizome six months or so beforehand. The back divisions, left undisturbed for this time, will be well-established with new growths before being disturbed. Give recently potted orchids more shade and generally try to protect them from stress until they become established.

These remarks about dividing plants apply to sympodial not monopodial orchids. Some kinds of sympodials benefit from different treatment in re-potting and propagating. There are genera that can be propagated from new plantlets that appear on canes or even flower stems. These will be mentioned in later chapters where the different kinds of orchids are described. In general, no orchid likes to be disturbed and re-potting usually results in a check in growth. It should not be done until really necessary.

Orchids from seed

Some plants taken from wild or vegetative divisions are often found in typical collections. Most will be plants raised from seed of parents in cultivation or perhaps mericlones of good orchids. Nowadays there is no reason why even the novice cannot have plants from seed produced in his or her own collection. It is an area where there is definitely such a thing as beginner's luck.

The classic formula for choosing the parents is to cross a good flower with a good flower. Rubbish crossed with rubbish will probably produce flowers of a similar quality. Typically, a hybridizer will mate a good flower with another which has that quality but may

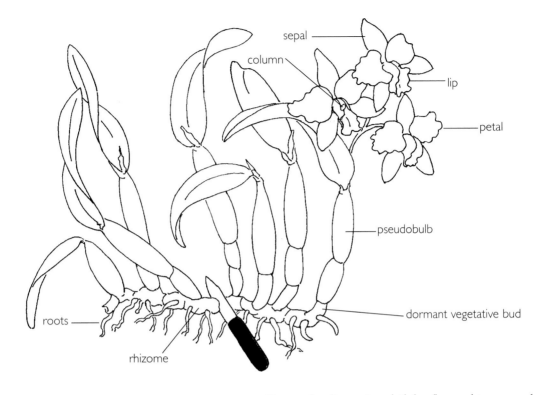

Where to divide a sympodial orchid – but best left until after flowering and new shoots and roots develop.

have a weakness in an area where the other parent is strong.

To make the cross, do it at about the time the seed parent's flower is a quarter to a third through its normal life. That is, if the flower would normally last about six weeks, do it when it has been open two weeks.

First, carefully remove the pollinia (pollen grains bound together in waxy masses) from the flower of the seed parent and take it away. Use a toothpick or sharpened match. Next, using a different toothpick, remove the pollinia from the pollen parent. It should be bright and yellow and waxy although some genera have dark pollinia. Press it well into the sticky stigmatic surface (if it is not fluid and sticky the flower may not be receptive) of the seed bearer. The stigma is the sticky cavity found on the undersurface of the organ formed by the union of the stamen, style and stigma of the flower.

Do not be disappointed if the flower dries up and drops off. Even if a seed capsule forms the seed may not be viable. Only a minority of pollinations are likely to succeed and the many reasons why they fail would fill more than a chapter in this book. Attempted crosses between widely unrelated genera are likely to fail.

If a seed capsule forms, the time taken for it to ripen is most likely to be between six months to a year, but will be a lot less in some genera. The capsule should be removed immediately if it starts to yellow. You can sow the seed yourself – it has been done on a kitchen sink – but it is usually a laboratory procedure. Instructions will be found in some orchid literature. Alternatively, the seed can be sent to one of the professional laboratories undertaking this work for hobbyists. Find out whether they prefer the dry seed or the capsule before it has split. If the seed is viable you should receive the seedlings back, ready to deflask, in six to 18 months.

Plants from flask

Seedlings need special care if they are to survive in the

39

Seedlings in a flask at a commercial laboratory.

real world outside the sterile flask. Remove them with a tool with a hook in the end (make one from wire) and drag them out roots first. If they cannot be removed that way, the flask will have to be broken. Fold it in a cloth or paper and hit it with a hammer. Wash the agar (the growing medium) off the roots in a bowl of lukewarm water. Plant the seedlings several

to a pot (termed *community pot*) and crowd them quite close as they like company at this stage. Sphagnum moss, shredded, can be tried but fine bark may be safer. If possible, first sterilize the bark in a pressure cooker.

An easy way to plant the community pot with bark is to place it in a bowl of water up to the rim. The seedlings can then be easily pushed down into the bark and will remain there when the pot is lifted up and drained. The seedlings should be put in low light and be exposed gradually to normal light intensity over three or four weeks. Keep the plants in a humid environment. An inverted clear glass or plastic container over the pot will help. Above all, apply a preventative fungicide as soon as potting has been completed and spray frequently, at least until they are well-established. Keep the pots in temperatures the adult plants are comfortable with.

If you cannot be bothered going through all this and have some seed, you might like to try the only method available to orchidists of old. This is to scatter the seed on the surface of a pot in which there is an established adult plant that has been in cultivation for some years. The surface of the medium should be firm and even have a growth of moss on top. Do not wash the seed off but immerse the pot in water up to the surface when necessary. Spray the top regularly with a fine spray of water. Growers who have had success with this method report that the seedlings so raised are unusually vigorous. Be warned, however, that this method of sowing only works occasionally.

Purchasing flasks

For most, the easiest way to acquire a lot of seedlings relatively cheaply is to purchase flasks from a reputable plant breeder. Such a vendor should have top-flight stud plants and the experience to know how to mate them to best advantage. Orchid magazines and catalogs will show that there is a large selection on the market. Many also sell community pots with the deflasked plants established and growing when you receive them.

Community pot. Plant flask seedlings this close together.

CHAPTER 9

Growing under Lights

Orchids in the home

Indoor orchid culture using window light was briefly mentioned in Chapter 4. Using a window facing the noon sun, with curtains to provide the appropriate light intensity, it is worth trying to grow almost any orchid. Where the orientation of the window is less favorable or where there is shading from trees or other buildings the choice is limited. Supplementary artificial lighting would again extend the possibilities.

If orchids are to be grown in a room that is usually occupied in the evenings, then high-intensity discharge (HID) lighting is not really suitable. The units are obtrusive and the color of the light can be distracting. In any event they are usually not needed. Where plants are receiving a modicum of sunlight for a very short period each day, fluorescent lamps will enable a wide range of orchids to be grown. Further, in this situation they need not be horticultural lamps with illumination of a distracting color. Cool white lamps are quite adequate unless perhaps the window does not get any sun at any time of the day.

A fixture with two 40-watt fluorescent lamps will be adequate in most situations. When and for how long the lamps should be on is a matter for fine judgment. Bear in mind that even outside the sun does not shine all day every day. Better to have the lamps on when in doubt but do not of course have them on when sunlight is coming through the window.

Humidity is often a problem. A common practice is to place the plants on, but not in, trays of gravel and water. Whether this will do much for humidity at leaf level is debatable.

In sunless rooms or basements orchids can be successfully cultivated entirely under artificial lights. But not any lights. The ordinary incandescent bulbs

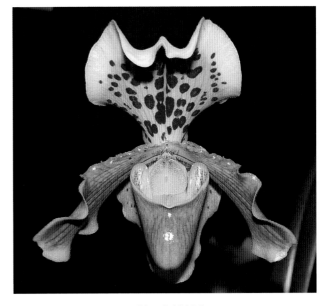

Paphiopedilum insigne var Harefield Hall

commonly used for household lighting do not, by themselves, usually provide enough of the right kind of light to grow plants satisfactorily.

Photosynthesis is heavily dependent upon radiation in specific wavelengths in the blue (short wavelength) and red (long wavelength) portions of the light spectrum. For optimum growth lamps are needed that provide an adequate amount of light output in these wavelengths. These are available as the well-known fluorescent tubes and as special and more powerful high-intensity discharge (HID) lamps.

When growing orchids under artificial lights, the plants require the same temperatures, pots, potting media and nutrients as they do under natural light but maintaining adequate humidity can be a problem in some circumstances. Spraying a lot of water around may not be acceptable in a living room! Many, however, manage it in a basement and enclose the area in plastic sheets to contain the humidity. Portable foggers (see Ch. 2) are available and may be helpful.

Day and night temperatures need to be monitored as most orchids must have a differential of at least 10 percent between day and night temperatures. You will need to cater to those plants that require seasonal drops to around 55°F (13°C) to initiate flowering.

Day length is important and entirely in your hands. At one time when cattleyas were more widely grown for cut flowers it was common practice to have fall-flowering plants flower out of season with artificial lights. Flowering was normally initiated by shortening days, but extending the daylight artificially tricked the plants into believing they were lengthening.

It is supposed that orchids growing naturally near the equator may not necessarily be influenced by day length. However, away from the equator many orchids flower once a year in nature, the flowering season determined by either shortening or lengthening days. When growing a mixed collection under lights the best policy is to follow the seasons outside, giving 16 to 18 hours light in summer and 10 to 12 hours in winter. The lights can be conveniently controlled by a time clock but daily adjustments are not necessary. Altering the day length every few weeks will work. Seasonal variation in day lengths is not essential for most non-flowering plants. Seedlings that have not reached flowering size benefit from long days year-round.

In days gone by, when artificial lighting was entirely based around fluorescent tubes, orchids with lower light requirements, such as *Phalaenopsis* and *Paphiopedilum*, were the most rewarding plants to grow. These days the more powerful lights available permit the culture of almost any orchid; but some still present difficulties.

Those with very high light requirements are best avoided. Very tall plants are also a problem. The energy in radiation from a single point source follows the inverse square law. Whatever the light energy received at the tip of the plant it can be only one quarter as strong at double the distance from the overhead light source.

The rate of attenuation can be lessened with reflectors over the light but, even so, if the tip of a tall plant such as a *Vanda* is receiving enough light the lower leaves will be under-illuminated. Strap-leafed vandas have been flowered successfully under lights but terete vandas that are both tall and need high light levels should not be grown under lights. Very large plants are not usually grown in these conditions. A *Cymbidium* with half a dozen flower stems may make a great display in spring but you could have 20 or so different minicatts in the same space with flowers year-round.

Fluorescent lights

A fluorescent tube has electrodes at each end and a phosphor coating on the inside of the glass. A discharge is struck between the electrodes and radiation from this discharge causes the phosphor coating to fluoresce. A relatively high voltage across the electrodes is required to initiate the discharge but a low voltage will then maintain it.

The components necessary to start the tubes and to then control the current through them is called the ballast. It is usually part of the permanent fixture into which the tubes are inserted. Fluorescent tubes are much more efficient than incandescent bulbs, consuming less electrical energy than the latter – i.e. they are cheaper to run for the same light output. The tubes run quite cool but the ballast will be warm and a fan or fans may be desirable in an enclosed area for ventilation and cooling.

The wavelengths or color of the light from a fluorescent tube depend upon the nature of the phosphor coating. Tubes emitting various colors are available and most manufacturers market a tube for horticultural purposes. Some of these tubes may not appear as bright as one might expect from the wattage. This is deceptive, as there is extra energy in the photosynthetically active parts of the light spectrum.

A bank of two 40-watt horticultural tubes is sufficient to grow orchids needing not much more than 1500 foot-candles. A more flexible set-up would have four 40-watt tubes spaced 4-6 in (10-15 cm) apart. The tubes should have some sort of reflector. They also should be of the horticultural type, but can

Masdevallia Jazz Time 'L & R'

disadvantage, not previously mentioned, is that the light output from fluorescent tubes falls as they age. As this happens, place the plants nearer the lights. Better still, try and have tubes of different ages running so they can be replaced one at a time.

HID lights

There are several types of high-intensity discharge lamps. The common two are high-pressure sodium lamps and metal halide lamps. Both will support plant growth but have somewhat different light spectrums, which are better balanced if the two are used together. Fixtures are available that have a high-pressure sodium lamp and a metal halide lamp in the same reflector. The advantage of HID lamps is their power, permitting the cultivation of plants with higher light requirements than can easily be provided by fluorescent tubes. They are available in powers of up to 1000 watts. The lamps need ballasts that, with the lamps, can get quite hot. A fan for ventilation and to cool the lamp and possibly the ballast is needed. Some lamps have the ballast in a separate unit that can be placed outside the growing area.

A 400-watt HID lamp with a suitable reflector will provide strong illumination over an area of about 16 sq ft (1.5 sq m). There will be an outer area of lesser illumination where plants with lower light requirements can be placed. This makes it easy to accommodate plants that need different light intensities in different seasons. For example *Dendrobium nobile* and its hybrids must be given stronger light at the end of summer if they are to flower the following spring.

HID lights are usually positioned about 27 in (70 cm) above the plants. One device on the market moves the light back and forth along a rail. The plants can then take turns to be closer to the lamp, exposing them to more intense light without burning. Many growers favor a set-up where a combination of HID and fluorescent tubes are used.

A disadvantage with HID lights is that they are more expensive to purchase and install than fluorescent tubes. If you are a beginner, it might be a good idea to experiment with fluorescent tubes first.

be mixed with cool white tubes for low-light plants or those not of flowering size. Some of the popular genera that can be grown and flowered under a set-up such as the above include *Phalaenopsis, Paphiopedilum, Miltoniopsis, Odontoglossum* (Colombian crispum kinds), *Disa* and *Masdevallia*. There are many others. These plants should be placed about 8 in (20 cm) below the lights or a little closer.

Orchids needing higher light levels – at least 2000 foot-candles – including compact plants in the cattleya alliance, can be flowered under fluorescents but must be placed as near the lights as possible without burning. Alternatively, provide more tubes spaced closer together.

Orchids needing 3000 foot-candles or more need HID lights. The foot-candles mentioned are those which an ordinary photographic light meter would indicate in sunlight (see p.18). Do not attempt to measure the radiation from horticultural lights in this way as the readings will be misleading.

A fluorescent light growing area is not too difficult to set up and can be relatively inexpensive. A

CHAPTER 10

The Cattleya Alliance

All these plants are members of the same sub-tribe of the orchid family, the Laeliinae, that comprises over 800 species in 43 genera.

A salient feature is the ease with which many of the genera can be crossed, one with another, resulting in a proliferation of intergeneric names. Although these hybrids tend to predominate in orchid collections, many of the species are grown for their own beauty. A selection of genera commonly in cultivation is listed. The cultural directions immediately below apply to cattleyas and the intergeneric hybrids with them. Where other genera can benefit from some modification of these conditions this is indicated either here or where these genera are individually discussed.

Culture

Temperature

Minimum night temperatures of about 55°F (12°C) will produce the best growth. It can go 4°F (2°C) lower when plants are not in active growth. *Sophronitis coccinea* and its hybrids will tolerate cooler temperatures. On the other hand, plants with *Cattleya dowiana* bloodlines will not. Mature plants need a 15-20°F (−9 − −7°C) difference between night and day. Maximum temperatures are not critical if the leaves do not overheat. Avoid strong drafts of cold air on opening flowers as they may collapse.

Housing

Cattleyas can be attached to, or hung under, trees in favorable areas such as Southern Florida and Hawaii. Even here, however, the best flowers often come from shade-houses with protection from

Sophrolaeliocattleya Orglade's Early Harvest 'Grace'

overhead rain so watering can be controlled. Further from the equator, cattleyas are usually grown indoors or in a greenhouse.

Light

Cattleyas can be grown on a window sill with filtered light for most of the day. In a shade-house or greenhouse 50 percent shade-cloth is appropriate. Under lights, about 2000 to 3000 foot-candles is normal – a little more if leaves are kept cool and a little less if they overheat. Leaves of an olive green color are getting all the light they need. The thick leaves are susceptible to sunburn.

Watering

The plants should be dried out between waterings. In cool, dull weather they will come to no harm if left dry for some days. Shriveling of the leading pseudobulbs suggests they are not getting enough water. A few wrinkles in the older pseudobulbs can be ignored. Nutrients are best included in the water with nitrogen at the 100 ppm level or less.

Potting

Keep these plants in as small a pot as possible. When re-potting, choose a pot that will allow for another two years' growth only. Do not over-pot. The best time to re-pot is when new roots are just emerging from the base of the leading growth. Be careful not to knock them off. When re-potting, ensure that the rhizome is not below the surface of the potting medium. Most cattleyas are grown in bark-based mixes these days.

Cattleya showing correct time for re-potting.

Propagation

Mature plants can be divided by cutting through the rhizomes, leaving divisions of about four pseudobulbs which can be potted separately. The back divisions will be incapable of making further roots but one of the dormant pseudobulbs can be coaxed into making a shoot with roots if kept in a warm, shady place. It will do so more certainly if the rhizome is cut and the plant is left in the pot and not re-potted until the old division shows signs of renewed growth. Reed stem epidendrums have branching stems with roots and pieces can be removed to propagate these plants. All members of the alliance can be tissue-cultured or raised from seed. If you acquire a seedling or mericlone that won't grow, or won't grow to flowering size, or won't flower at all, discard it. These plants occasionally appear among seedlings or mericlones and are useless.

Pests and diseases

Watch out for aphids, mealybug and scale. The tiny root-nibbling snail likes these plants. Most diseases that trouble other orchids are seen in the cattleya alliance and should be dealt with in the same way. Cattleya buds may rot in the flower sheath before emerging. All is likely to be well if the sheath is green but if it starts to yellow, remove it. To do this, first cut it off above the buds and the rest is easy.

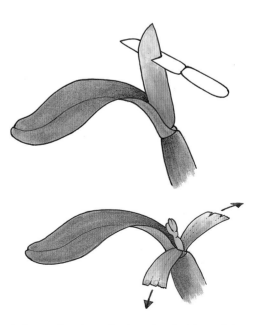

A flower sheath on *Cattleya* showing signs of decay must be opened up immediately before buds rot too.

Sophrolaelia Pole Star 'Spotlight'

Brassavola

There are about 15 tropical American species.

Brassavola (Rhyncholaelia) digbiana. Although not widely cultivated now, this orchid from Central America is historically famous for being widely used by early hybridizers to create the intergeneric hybrids *Brassocattleya* and *Brassolaeliocattleya*. Their idea was to incorporate the spectacular fringed lip into hybrids. The flowers are large and greenish and can be grown with cattleyas.

Broughtonia

A West Indian genus of one or two species, although some authorities recognize more.

Broughtonia sanguinea. A medium-sized plant with many showy crimson flowers borne on long stems in fall and winter. Line breeding has produced beautifully colored round flowers up to 1¹/₂ in (4 cm) in diameter. Yellow and white forms have been discovered. This is a lowland tropical orchid but can be grown the same way as cattleyas. It does like plenty of light and dislikes wet roots. For the latter reason it does well if established on a slab. The species has been crossed with other members of the cattleya alliance and some very beautiful hybrids are available.

Cattleya

A genus of 30 to 50 species depending upon how some of them are classified. The thickened stems, or pseudobulbs, have one or two, rarely more, thick leaves at the top. The flowers arise from a terminal lead and are in many kinds protected by a sheath.

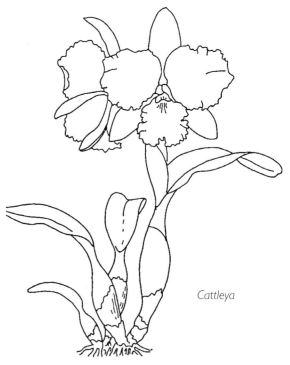

Cattleya

Cattleya aclandiae. A dwarfish plant bearing one or two 3 in (8 cm) flowers of heavy substance. The base color is green or brown but heavily blotched with purple. The rhizomes are long, so the plant quickly grows out of a pot. For this reason it is often grown on a slab. It likes to be dried out quickly between waterings and prefers minimum temperatures of 60°F (15°C).

Cattleya labiata. This species has club-shaped pseudobulbs up to 10 in (25 cm) tall, bearing one leaf. The flowers, one to five in number, emerge from a sheath or a sheath within a sheath. They are large, about 5¹/₂ in (14 cm) in diameter. The color is variable from white through pale pink to magenta.

Sophrolaeliocattleya Medley 'L'

Similar species (some have been occasionally regarded as variants within a single species) include *C. dowiana* (a yellow), *C. mendelii*, *C. mossiae*, *C. trianae*, *C. warneri* and *C. warscewiczii*. All these have showy flowers and are, or used to be, what most people could identify as an orchid. The magnificent large-flowered cattleyas found in orchid collections today have these bloodlines and may have a family tree going back 100 years.

Cattleya luteola. This is a dwarf plant with clustered pseudobulbs and 2 in (5 cm) yellow flowers clustered on a short stem. Not common in cultivation but, mated with *Sophronitis coccinea,* produced the very successful hybrid *Sophrocattleya* Beaufort.

Cattleya walkeriana. Compared with the labiata section this is a smallish plant. An unusual feature, for cattleyas, is that the flower stem arises not from the terminal bud at the top of the pseudobulb but from the base of the pseudobulb. The flowers,

typically two to a stem, are relatively large at 3 in (8 cm) across, of good substance and quite showy. Typical color is in shades of purple but pure whites are also seen. It is one parent, with *Laelia pumila,* of the much-awarded hybrid *Laeliocattleya* Mini Purple. Line breeding has developed some fine forms of this species. The long rhizomes are a disadvantage, making for a rambling plant that quickly grows over the side of a pot. It flowers in winter.

Encyclia

These are mainly epiphytic plants with a growth habit similar to cattleyas but tend to be smaller plants with smaller flowers and shorter pseudobulbs. They have suffered from name changes by botanists. They used to be epidendrums or cattleyas and now some are yet again being transferred, this time to a genus called *Prosthechea*. Encyclias can be grown as cattleyas, although many like cooler conditions.

There are many species, but all in the selection below are quite showy and well worth growing. These three come from Mexico and will accept cooler conditions than cattleyas.

Encyclia (Cattleya) citrina. A high-altitude spring- and summer-flowering species growing at altitudes of up to 7200 ft (2200 m). The pseudobulbs and leaves have a silvery gray appearance and the plant tends to grow downward with pendulous flower stems. For this reason it is easier to manage on a slab. The flowers are fragrant and golden yellow, borne singly, but they do not open fully. It needs to be kept fairly dry in winter.

Encyclia mariae. The plant looks like an upright growing *Encyclia citrina* but the flowers are quite different. These have glossy jade-green sepals and petals and a large white lip. The 2$^1/_4$ in (6 cm) fully open flowers come two to four on a stem in summer. The color of the flowers is quite striking and the plant always attracts attention when exhibited.

Encyclia (Prosthechea) vitellina. A species, bright orange-red with a yellow lip, found growing at elevations of up to 6500 ft (2000 m). About a dozen 1$^1/_2$ in (4 cm) flowers open sequentially on 8 in (20 cm) stems in late summer.

Epidendrum

There are hundreds of species, more than any other genus in the cattleya alliance. The plants are epiphytic or lithophytic, some even being terrestrial. Most lack swollen pseudobulbs. Their natural habitat extends from the Carolinas in North America down to Argentina and their requirements in cultivation are somewhat varied. The examples given below are both popular species but with quite different flowers.

Epidendrum pseudoepidendrum. Tall, slender stems with the leaves all on the upper portion. The 2$^1/_4$ in (6 cm) flowers are of heavy substance with an almost plastic appearance. The color is spectacular, with green sepals and petals contrasting with a large

bright orange lip. This species will grow with cattleyas but enjoys slightly higher temperatures. However, it will tolerate minimums of 55°F (12°C).

Epidendrum radicans. This plant has long (39 in or 1 m), thin stems with many aerial roots. Clusters of 1$^1/_2$ in (4 cm) flowers are borne on terminal elongating stems. Flower size is variable, as is color, which is commonly orange or red. *E. ibaguense* is a similar or the same species but there are others, all referred to as reed stem epidendrums. *E. radicans* is classified as a warm-grower but is fairly tolerant temperature-wise. In frost-free areas it can be grown in the garden in full sun. Where there are only light frosts, and the air temperature does not go below zero, it can be tried under a tree or against the wall of a building protected by the eaves of the roof, but

Laelia sincorana

Laeliocattleya and *Sophrolaeliocattleya*. However, many of the species are widely grown for their own qualities and a few popular ones are listed below. Except where indicated, or if in doubt, give them the same cultural conditions as cattleyas.

Laelia anceps. An epiphytic or lithophytic species from Mexico with four-sided pseudobulbs and up to six flowers on a long stem. The weight of the flowers bends the stem to a semi-pendulous position – they are displayed best like this and so no attempt should be made to stake the stem upright. The flowers may be up to 4 in (10 cm) in diameter and are typically rose-purple but there are other color variations, including pure white. Flowers in winter or spring. The plant likes good light and cooler conditions than cattleyas. It is a good plant for beginners and a popular plant with many growers. It will tolerate temperatures down to 40°F (4°C) in winter.

Laelia lundii. An interesting small species from Brazil with stems of one to three white, rose-tipped flowers. The flowers come up with heavy, cylindrical leaves in spring and open before the leaf is fully developed. This orchid will not flower unless the plant is kept quite dry through the winter months.

Laelia purpurata. The national flower of Brazil. It is an epiphyte and a larger plant than any of the other laelias mentioned here, being up to 20 in (50 cm) high. There are up to five 6 in (15 cm) flowers on a stem. The color is typically pink but many color forms exist, including white petals and sepals with lips of various colors. The species is widely line bred by Brazilian hobbyists and literature catalogs over 100 different varieties, with some reported to change hands at high prices. This species flowers from late spring to fall.

it must not be in shade for more than an hour or two each day. It needs quick-draining material around the roots. In the greenhouse it can be grown in pots in the peat-based mix suggested for cymbidiums but the medium should be watered before it has quite dried out. In good strong light it will provide a display of flowers for months. Unsuitable for the home, even under lights.

Laelia

Some 50 or more species are found over a wide area from Central to South America. The plants and growth habit are very similar to *Cattleya*, and the greenhouses of the world are awash with fine inter-generic hybrids bearing laelia bloodlines, particularly

Rupicolous laelias. Rupicolous means growing on rocks and that is what this group of species does, in Brazil, some in full sun. They are relatively small plants and most bear several flowers on longish stems. The leaves are upright, ending in a sharp point, said to have evolved as a deterrent to grazing animals. They are spring-flowering but often flower at other times in cultivation. There seems to be at least 40 species in this section, some only recently introduced into cultivation, and they are well worth a place in any collection. These orchids are not difficult to grow if given good light and a medium that dries out fairly quickly after watering. The deep yellow *Laelia briegeri* is one of the most beautiful species, with 2¼ in (6 cm) flowers with wider sepals and petals than others in the section. It has been the parent of some colorful hybrids. Two rather similar plants, *L. lucasiana* and *L. longipes*, have marginally smaller magenta flowers with yellow lips. A great conversation piece is the tiny *L. lilliputiana*, only 2¼ in or 6 cm tall, with rose-colored flowers. It is in fact one of the smallest plants in the entire cattleya alliance.

Sophronitis

This genus is surely the jewel in the crown of the cattleya alliance. The plants are miniature and the salient feature is the brilliant color of the flowers. They are widely grown for their own beauty but have been extensively used in hybridization in attempts to create large, red-flowered cattleyas. Some of the many sophrolaeliocattleyas and other combinations of genera are close to achieving this. The majority of the popular mini-catts have this genus in their bloodlines. There are seven species, all easily recognized as belonging to the genus.

Sophronitis cernua. This is the most distinctive member of the genus. It is a smaller plant than the others and bears two to five 1 in (2.5 cm) orange-red flowers on a spike. It seems to do well on a slab.

Sophronitis coccinea. This used to be called *Sophronitis grandiflora*. The 3 in (8 cm) high plants bear bright scarlet flowers that are large (2¼ in/6 cm) in relation to the size of the plant, though flowers much larger than this, resulting from line breeding, have been exhibited. The flowers emerge with the developing leaf in spring. The species grows in Brazil

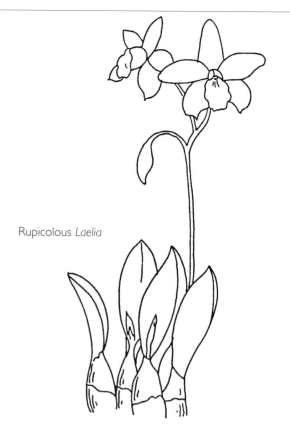

Rupicolous *Laelia*

as an epiphyte in damp rainforests in partial shade. In cultivation it should not be allowed to dry out completely in summer, but needs watering with discretion as the roots will decay if kept permanently wet. These plants reach flowering size in 2 in (5 cm) pots. An effort should be made to keep them in small pots as it seems to take much skill to maintain the plants in good condition in pots larger than 3 in (7.5 cm).

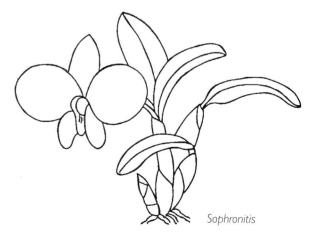

Sophronitis

Above: *Sophronitis coccinea* '109 FTF' Below: *Cattleya* Angelwalker

CHAPTER 11

Cymbidium

Benjamin Samuel Williams was the author of one of the best 19th-century books on orchid culture. In his 1877 edition of *The Orchid Growers Manual* he prefaced the few words he had to say about cymbidiums with these words:

"There are several species of this genus, but only a few that are admissible into a choice selection of orchidaceous plants."

Some important species had not been discovered when Mr. Williams wrote this, but he would nevertheless have been astounded by the modern hybrids we have today. Modern standard hybrids have from eight to 20 or more flowers on stems which may be erect, arching or pendulous. They are of quite heavy substance and come in pale pink through mauve to near-red plus pure whites, yellow and greens. Being better able to stand the stress of storage and trans-

Above: *Cymbidium* (Hallmark x Balcariga)
Opposite: *Cymbidium* Rae James 'Topaz'

portation, cymbidiums are widely grown for cut flowers and are popular with florists.

The so-called standard cymbidiums are quite large plants with strap-like leaves and prominent pseudobulbs. They have been bred from cooler-growing species native to the foothills of the Himalayas. Shortly after World War II hybrids started to be produced based on a smaller compact plant previously little-used in breeding. This was *Cymbidium floribundum*, previously known as *C. pumilum*.

We now have many beautiful hybrids with smaller flowers on compact, smallish plants, some incorporating the bloodlines of a few other miniature species. They are known as miniatures and are popular because they take up less room and flower earlier (from midwinter) than the standards.

Culture
Potting
Cymbidiums are best grown in pots or tubs. Mixes based on pine bark seem to be the most popular

potting media. However, the plants grow well in the peat-based medium described in Chapter 5.

Temperature and light

Cymbidiums enjoy night temperatures of 50-60°F (10-15°C), though they will tolerate temperatures down to 40°F (5°C). In cool-summer areas that don't have heavy frosts, these orchids can be grown as garden plants. Daytime temperatures of 70-85°F (21-30°C) are ideal. Minimum winter temperatures of 50°F (10°C) are ideal for the best quality flowers from plants in a greenhouse. Plants grown in shade-houses or outside will survive light frosts but if there are flower spikes or buds at this time these could be damaged. Cymbidiums are difficult plants under artificial light. They are too large. Under lights, intensities of 4000 foot-candles are desirable but could go down to 3000 foot-candles in greenhouses if necessary to keep temperatures down.

Shade-cloth of 30 percent to 50 percent is satisfactory for shade-houses. Miniature cymbidiums are the best to try under lights due to the smaller size.

Housing

The best plants and flowers seem to come more often from greenhouse culture. Cymbidiums will nevertheless grow well outside or in shade-houses in frost-free areas, but, they really need overhead protection from rain when in flower. Many hobbyists succeed by putting the plants outside under a tree and bringing them under cover to a porch or sunny room in early winter or when the flower stems are developing. Select an outside position where full sun is received early and late in the day and filtered light at other times. These plants will of course be more difficult to protect from insects, slugs and snails.

Below: *Cymbidium* Legacy 'Conference'

Watering and nutrition

When strong growth is being made in late spring and summer, cymbidiums need plenty of water and benefit from a slightly higher amount of nutrients in the water supply. In winter let the plants almost, but not quite, dry out between waterings.

Pests and diseases

Well-grown plants are not particularly susceptible to diseases but watch for viruses and the spoiling of flowers by fungal spotting from having humidity too high and too little air movement when temperatures are low. A serious pest is the two-spotted mite which can proliferate with alarming speed in hot summer weather. It pays to be vigilant and deal with these pests before numbers build up.

Flowering

The cooler-growing, large-flowered species from the Himalayan foothills predominate in the bloodlines of standard cymbidium hybrids. These plants are difficult to flower in the tropics, probably because temperatures are not cold enough or there is not enough differentiation between day and night at the time flowers are initiated. In temperate climates, where the cultivation of cymbidiums is popular, flowering seems to be initiated through summer. That is when the plant decides whether or not it is going to flower in the following spring, although flower spikes may not be seen until later. Minimum temperatures at this season are not usually particularly low, suggesting there may be other factors involved. Light is undoubtably one.

Occasionally one sees a collection of cymbidiums shut up in a tiny greenhouse in the middle of summer with the temperatures inside high enough to threaten human survival. The plants look ready to expire, their leaves sad and yellow, and the owner is given some well-meaning advice. But spring comes, the plants are still there and the greenhouse is a mass of flowering plants. At the other extreme people put cymbidiums out under shady trees in summer and complain that the plants don't flower.

If your plants are reluctant to flower look first to light levels. Providing enough light in the home may

Cymbidium

be a problem. Dark green, limp foliage suggests too little light. Move to a south-facing window or consider using artificial lights (see Chapter 9). To this end let the leaf temperatures go quite high if necessary. Reducing the nitrogen in the feeding program will help but should not be required. Plants in flower should be given much lower light levels to preserve flower quality and longevity.

Species

There are about 50 species growing over a wide geographical area from the Himalayan foothills to China, Japan and Taiwan and down to Indonesia and Australia. Some are tropical, some from cooler climates, often due to altitude, some are epiphytic and some are terrestrial. Unfortunately the cooler-growing species on which our standard cymbidiums were founded are now not so often seen in cultivation. Those listed below are often found in collections. They come from varied climates, but will generally succeed when grown with other cymbidiums.

Cymbidium canaliculatum. A plant with rigid, thick leaves and clustered pseudobulbs. Long, arching stems bear many 1¹/₂ in (4 cm) flowers with brown, purple or dull red sepals and petals with a creamy white, red-marked lip. Recently, a variety with pure green petals and sepals and a contrasting white lip was brought into cultivation in Australia. This is an attractive flower. It is being propagated and should become more readily available. In nature, *C. canaliculatum* shuns moist coastal and mountain areas and is found in the drier western side of the Great Dividing Range down the eastern coast of Australia. It is typically found on partly hollow branches or on rotten logs with the roots penetrating these and not exposed. Its habitat is low rainfall areas in good light and often in full sun. In cultivation this species is best treated as an epiphyte, with the same potting medium as for cattleyas and drying the medium out between waterings. It must have strong light and infrequent watering during the winter months.

Cymbidium devonianum. This species is found growing as an epiphyte or lithophyte in the Himalayan foothills. It has wide, leathery leaves with little in the way of a pseudobulb and to the uninitiated it might not be recognized as a cymbidium when not in flower. The pendulous flower stems bear 1¹/₄ in (3 cm) flowers in shades of green, red and brown. The inflorescence will grow down well below the bottom of the container and, in common with most pendulous cymbidiums, the pot must be suspended when the plant is in flower. Again, in common with the others, no attempt should be made to stake the flower stems upright when they are developing. They will not elongate in this position, resulting in short stems and bunched flowers. *C. devonianum* can be cultivated similarly to other cymbidiums. It is not a large plant and appears in the ancestry of many miniature cymbidiums.

Below: *Cymbidium* (Hallmark × Balcariga) 'FTF'

Cymbidium ensifolium. It might be easier to say where this wide-ranging species does not grow, as it appears in most countries where other cymbidiums are found. It is a largely terrestrial species of modest size bearing 12 fragrant 2 in (5 cm) flowers, green or greenish-brown in color, in late summer or fall. It has made its mark in hybridization by being a parent of the tetraploid *Cym.* Peter Pan 'Greensleeves'. This orchid has, in turn, been responsible for extending the flowering season of modern hybrids by producing some attractive progeny which flower in mid- to late summer. Flowers from most of these hybrids do not last well when cut and are best admired on the plant.

Cym. sinense is a similar species, and both have been used to produce temperature-tolerant hybrids that will flower in the tropics. Most of this type of breeding is being pioneered in Florida.

Cymbidium suave. This Australian species grows mostly as an epiphyte on eucalyptus trees in Australia from the Tropic of Capricorn down to the Victorian border, a range of some 12° of latitude. It is a miniature plant, as cymbidiums go, with thin, stiff leaves about 20 in (50 cm) high and no pseudobulbs. In late spring the pendulous flower stems bear $^3/_4$ in (2 cm) flowers in shades of green, some with a brushing of brown.

It is a charming species that should be more widely cultivated, though it seems to be somewhat more appreciated outside its native Australia. Needing good light and a quick-draining potting medium, it resents being disturbed and should be left in the same pot as long as possible. The ideal temperature required probably depends upon where, in its wide climate range, your particular plant came from. In general this species will usually grow with other cymbidiums. Do not attempt to tear off the old dead leaf bases, as one would with other cymbidiums, as part of the living tissue is likely to be damaged.

Cymbidium tigrinum. One of the smallest plants in the genus, being about 8 in (20 cm) high, with wide leaves and small, round, clustered pseudobulbs. It is another member of the genus which does not look like a typical cymbidium when not in flower. The short flower stems bear about three 2 in (5 cm) flowers which are dull, yellowish-green with a white lip. The flowers are more interesting than the description of them might suggest. This species is a cool-grower and can be cultivated in all respects like standard cymbidiums. Flowers open in late spring. There are a few attractive hybrids with the white lip often predominant.

CHAPTER 12

Dendrobium

There are perhaps over 1000 species in this sympodial genus, making it one of the largest in the orchid family. The geographical range is also large, being much the same as cymbidiums, except that it extends into the islands of the South Pacific, growing from sea level to considerable altitudes. There is such a diversity of vegetative and floral structure it is difficult to generalize. But one common feature is that the flowers have a more or less prominent spur formed by the base of the lower sepals and lip over a column foot.

The genus has been classified into a number of different sections. Space does not permit a discussion of other than the seven sections below, but the majority of the species of horticultural importance are included in these. As could be expected the cultural requirements of this diverse group vary somewhat. If in doubt, the best approach is to treat them in all respects as if they were cattleyas but with a little higher light intensity. Dropping of leaves in the winter suggests those particular plants should be kept quite dry during this season.

Section *Callista*

A small section of Asian species with deep green leaves of good substance confined to the upper portion of swollen canes. These can be grown in the same way as cattleyas, including minimum temperatures of 50°F (10°C), but require less water in winter. A few hybrids have been made, but species are more common in collections. The examples below are all spring-flowering.

Top right: *Dendrobium* Malones 'Victory'. Opposite: *Dendrobium* (Penny Rose x Blushing Rose) x *kingianum*

Dendrobium densiflorum. A 12 in (30 cm) four-angled pseudobulb plant with a stem carrying many yellow 2 in (5 cm) flowers with fringed lips. Spectacular in flower, but the blooms are not particularly long-lasting.

Dendrobium palpebrae. A similar plant to the one above but the flowers are white with some orange in the lip.

Dendrobium trigonopus. Waxy, 2 in (5 cm) yellow flowers with a green base to the lip. The glistening flowers are spectacular and immediately attract attention.

Dendrobium Berry 'Oda'

Section *Dendrocoryne*

Orchids from this section grow naturally on the coast on the wetter side of the great dividing range in eastern Australia. They are epiphytes or lithophytes with leaves of good substance on the top of pseudobulbs that are relatively slender and wider at the bottom. An enormous amount of hybridizing has been done with this section in Australia and many attractive hybrids of great horticultural merit are now being seen both within this section and incorporating other sections. The three species below are commonly cultivated and line breeding within each of these has given us some flowers of superior form and color. Grow in bark-based media.

Dendrobium falcorostrum. This one is definitely a cool-growing orchid, appearing naturally as an epiphyte in the great dividing range in eastern Australia at elevations above 3300 ft (1000 m) in cool, moist, cloud forest. This area often experiences light dustings of snow in winter. The near-terminal racemes bear many fragrant, pristine white flowers about 1¹/₂ in (4 cm) across in spring. It will grow in the same potting medium as the others in this

section. It is reported to do particularly well on a slab of tree fern. As a cool-grower it dislikes high daytime temperatures. However, it still needs high light – even full sun – in winter. *D. falcorostrum* is one of the most beautiful species in this section.

Dendrobium kingianum. A common, easily-grown orchid, mainly lithophytic in nature. The size of the plant can vary from 2 in (5 cm) to as much as 20 in (50 cm) high but is commonly about 8 in (20 cm), with the inflorescence of six or so flowers arising from a bud at or near the top of the pseudobulb. The flowers are up to 1¹/₂ in (4 cm) across. Color can be from white through pink to deep mauve. They prefer an altitude of about 1000 ft (300 m) in nature but have been found growing up to 4000 ft (1200 m).

These orchids like good light and can be grown in the same medium as for cattleyas. In hot summer months they should not quite dry out between waterings but must be kept drier over fall and winter months to encourage flowering in spring.

They may make aerial growths or keikis (a Hawaiian name for babies) that will produce roots and these can be removed and potted or left on the plant to flower. *D. kingianum* will tolerate temperatures down to almost freezing without coming to any harm. It is one of the few orchids that often succeeds in the hands of someone who otherwise knows nothing about the cultivation of this plant family.

Dendrobium speciosum. By far the largest plant in this section. Two to six leathery leaves and long racemes with up to 80 densely packed, 2 in (5 cm), or larger, white to yellow flowers. A large plant in flower is spectacular. This is a variable species that is found in Australia from northern Queensland down to Victoria, a distance of some 3000 miles (5000 km) north to south. Southern forms are quite cool-growers and should be grown much the same as *D. kingianum*. However, the species does like plenty of light, and it can be left outside in full sun where it will tolerate light frosts but needs shelter from wind and rain to preserve the flowers.

Dendrobium tetragonum. A rather variable species with a wide latitude range. The pseudobulbs are thin at the base and thicker and four-angled at the top, where the weight often results in pendulous growths. The length of these is as variable as *D. kingianum*. Two to four greenish or yellowish, spidery, 5 in (12 cm) flowers are borne on short stems. Flowers in spring. Some northern forms can flower at any time, but these like higher minimum temperatures. This plant is an epiphyte. Intervals between waterings should be increased in winter even to the point of a slight shriveling of the pseudobulbs.

Section *Eugenanthe*

Plants in this section are sometimes referred to as soft cane dendrobiums, although the term is a little misleading. The plants mentioned below are all epiphytes, and they will survive winter night temperatures down to 37°F (3°C) if kept dry.

Dendrobium pseudoglomeratum

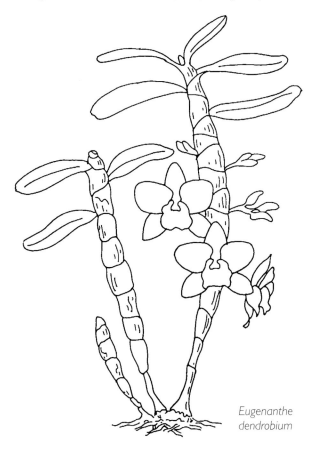

Eugenanthe dendrobium

Dendrobium nobile. The species grows naturally from the Himalayas down as far as Vietnam at elevations up to 4000 ft (1200 m). Finger-thick canes, up to 20 in (50 cm) high, tend to drop their leaves when mature and in spring bear flowers as large as 3 in (8 cm) across, in clusters of up to three, from the upper nodes. Temperatures near freezing are not a problem in cultivation, nor is warm or even hot summer weather. Flowers are in shades of pink to purple and there is a white form (var *virginalis*). They can be potted using the same medium as for cattleyas. Longer canes tend to be pendulous and are usually staked upright to give the best flower display.

There are quite strict rules to observe if this species is to produce flowers in spring. During summer, water frequently and ensure that they do not lack nutrients. During this time about 3000 foot-candles of light is adequate (see p. 17). From early fall, decrease the watering frequency and cease giving them any nitrogenous fertilizer – but continue to feed them with phosphorus and potassium. At this time the plants require much more light, even full sunlight. From the onset of winter, cease giving any nutrients

Propagation of *Dendrobium nobile* and hybrids. Simply remove and pot adventitious growth as in A. If mature cane is removed too, as in B, propagation will reach flowering size sooner.

and water only to arrest any shriveling of the canes. Normal watering and nutrition can be resumed when flower buds appear. Failure to observe the rules will result in long canes that produce aerial growths or keikis instead of flowers. These can be removed and potted when they develop roots.

Nobile hybrids. Over 100 years of hybridization, occasionally incorporating other species, has given us tetraploid plants with thicker, shorter canes and larger, more shapely, long-lasting flowers. These modern plants have blooms of considerable beauty and are now often referred to as Yamamoto hybrids. Mr. Yamamoto, in Japan, has done more to bring them to perfection than any other of his predecessors of earlier times.

These hybrids should be grown in the same way as *Dendrobium nobile* species.

Dendrobium aphyllum. A widespread, showy, Southeast Asian species with long, pendulous canes. The mature canes drop their leaves in winter and produce 2 in (5 cm) white to mauve flowers along the length of the cane in spring. This species can be grown the same way as nobile dendrobiums but does appreciate slightly higher minimum winter temperatures (50°F/10°C). *D. pierardii* is a very similar, perhaps the same, species.

Dendrobium fimbriatum. A cool- to warm-growing species found in Southeast Asia. Many 2 in (5 cm) flowers are borne on long, leafless canes in spring. The flowers are golden yellow with a pretty fringed lip. Treat much like nobile dendrobiums, but some water is needed during the winter months.

Dendrobium heterocarpum (aureum). A widespread and variable species. Most varieties in cultivation are cool-growing and should be given *Dendrobium nobile* treatment in the winter, when they drop their leaves before flowering from leafless canes in early spring. The flowers are 2 in (5 cm) across and are pale yellow. This species appears in the early ancestry of yellow nobile-type hybrids.

Section *Nigrohirsutae*

This Asian section has deep green leaves and stout canes, which are covered with black or brown hairs. They can be grown with the same light levels and potting media as cattleyas. A humid atmosphere is desirable. Temperature requirements vary with the species. Flowers in this section come in winter and spring and have white petals and sepals and, although they appear somewhat papery, they are quite long-lasting. Hybrids within the section have been made but the species mentioned below are all attractive plants and are quite common in collections. These are evergreen dendrobiums – they do not drop their leaves in winter and do not have to be kept dry during this season.

Dendrobium bellatulum. This is a dwarfish member of the section with canes about 4 in (10 cm) high.

The flowers are up to 1½ in (4 cm) wide with a colorful red-orange lip. Fairly cool-growing with minimum winter temperatures of 50°F (10°C). A similar but even smaller species is *D. margaritaceum*.

Dendrobium formosum. This one is related to *D. infundibilum* but, although it has been found growing at high elevations, plants in cultivation seem to need warmer minimum night temperatures (54°F/12°C) for best results. Canes are up to 18 in (45 cm) long and bear starry white flowers larger than those of the other two species described here.

Dendrobium infundibilum. Originally found at quite high elevations, this species is a cool-grower with canes typically about 16 in (40 cm) high and 3 in (8 cm) or larger flowers borne towards the apex of matured growths. Quite common in cultivation. *D. jamesianum* is a similar, or perhaps the same, species.

Section *Oxyglossum*

Orchids in this section are small plants native to Irian Jaya and Papua New Guinea or outlying islands with a few extending to the Pacific. Some species have been brought into cultivation only fairly recently. They are high-altitude plants that rarely survive if brought down to sea level within the tropical latitudes where they are found. They are not difficult to cultivate in temperate climates where they are still definitely cool-growers, withstanding temperatures down to near freezing but disliking intense dry summer heat. In summer, frequent misting and good air movement will help, but shade them more if necessary to keep leaf temperatures down. Some species in this section occasionally grow in full sunshine in nature but be cautious about subjecting the plants to this in cultivation.

There are about 28 species in the section. They tend to have "upside down" flowers, with the lip uppermost. Those mentioned below may all be grown under similar conditions. As to potting media, almost everything including sphagnum moss has been tried. In nature the plants alternately

Dendrobium cuthbertsonii

become wet and dry daily so a quick-drying medium is important. The safest is probably a bark-based mix as for cattleyas, but do not let any of them remain dry at the roots for more than a day at the most. Firm rules for the successful cultivation of oxyglossums have not yet been agreed upon so do not be afraid to experiment. A handful of hybrids involving this section exist, but they are not yet widely distributed.

Dendrobium cuthbertsonii. *D. sophronites* was the name originally given to this species by the botanist Schlecter because it reminded him of the unrelated *Sophronitis coccinea* from Brazil. This is the gem in the crown of the genus with flowers that last in perfection for six months or even longer.

The plants are small, about 2 in (5 cm) high, with leaves of heavy substance on top of small pseudobulbs. The flowers give the appearance of being almost larger than the plants, up to 1 in (3 cm) across and a 2 in (5 cm) pot can have a dozen flowers. The common color is scarlet or orange, but there are yellow and pink or magenta forms and bicolors with a combination of two distinct colors. Not found in other orchids are the dense prominent warts on the upper surface of the leaves, the purpose of which is not clear.

Dendrobium cuthbertsonii

Dendrobium cuthbertsonii grows in Irian Jaya and Papua New Guinea at altitudes of up to 10,000 ft (3000 m). It is an epiphyte, on moss-covered trees in quite heavy shade and even as a kind of terrestrial in the open on high-altitude grassland. This suggests it may be able to adapt to a wide range of conditions in cultivation. Particularly fine plants have been grown on tree-fern slabs. Plants raised from seed tend to be easier to grow than those removed from their native habitat. The two-spotted mite likes this species and can literally destroy plants. It is impossible to spray under the leaves. Invert the pot and dip the foliage in a miticide.

Dendrobium laevifolium. A compact, 4 in (10 cm) high plant with usually two leaves atop flask-shaped pseudobulbs. The flowers arise from leafless older bulbs at any time of the year but particularly in fall in cultivation. Most of the plants in cultivation are from Rossel Island, east of Papua New Guinea, and the flowers are deep rose or mauve in color – about the same size as *D. cuthbertsonii* or a little larger.

Plants with lighter colors, or even white flowers, have been reported from Bougainville, the Solomon Islands, Vanuatu and elsewhere. This is a pretty species, somewhat less demanding in cultivation than *D. cuthbertsonii*.

Dendrobium prasinum. This species deserves to be grown more widely. It is similar to *D. laevifolium* but the deep green leaves have more substance and the flowers are white. It grows naturally in the islands of Fiji.

Dendrobium sulphureum. A variable species. The plant is about 4 in (10 cm) high, with several leaves on the upper half of thin, cylindrical, clustered pseudobulbs bearing one or two flowers up to 1 in (2.5 cm) long. The flowers are yellow or yellow-green with a striking, contrasting, orange lip. This is a pretty species and can be grown the same way as other oxyglossums.

Opposite: *Dendrobium sulphureum* on a dead branch in a high-altitude Papua New Guinea rainforest.

Dendrobium vexillarius. This is the most abundant of all the Irian Jaya species in this section and is found as an epiphyte in a wide range of habitats (up to over 10,000 ft or 3000 m), in color forms from blue to dark crimson. A somewhat taller plant than the others mentioned here, *D. vexillarius* has slender pseudobulbs, swollen at the base, with two or three leaves on top.

The flowers, up to 1½ in (4 cm) wide, are borne in clusters of several flowers, more than one flower stem often coming from the same node at the top of the bulb. Some growers find this species easy to grow but others say it is difficult. The reason for this is not clear, but it is a worthwhile plant to have. Try giving it the same conditions as other oxyglossums.

Section *Phalaenanthe*

There are only a few species in this section but two are very important – *Dendrobium phalaenopsis* and *D. biggibum*. Both are often regarded as the same species. They are found in the north of eastern Australia and in Papua New Guinea and Indonesia. The canes are typically about 12 in (30 cm) high, but can be much higher. They are cylindrical and slightly swollen in the middle, with a few leathery

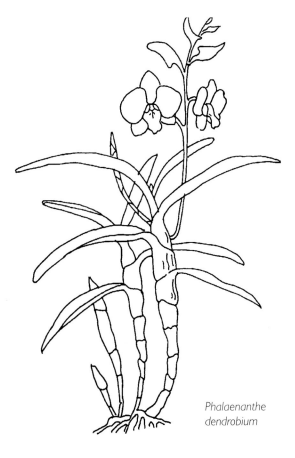

Phalaenanthe dendrobium

leaves at the top. The flower stem has many 2 in (5 cm) or larger, long-lasting flowers in white or shades of pink through to intense, deep purple. *D. biggibum*, the Cooktown orchid, is the state flower of the state of Queensland, Australia. The shape of the flowers is reminiscent of the quite unrelated genus *Phalaenopsis*, the moth orchid.

These plants come from areas with hot, wet summers and somewhat drier winters and this indicates their requirements in cultivation. They must be dried quickly between watering in all seasons, and need a quick-draining potting medium. Keep them in as small a pot as possible. The plants can stand quite high light intensities. Grown indoors, they will survive with minimum night temperatures of 50°F (10°C), but for best growth and flower quality in the fall they really need minimums of nearer 60°F (15°C) all year. These are tropical orchids.

The plants in cultivation labelled *Dendrobium phalaenopsis* will probably have been the product of line breeding over several generations with flowers of impressive size, conformation and color. Much hybridizing with other sections has been done, particularly with section *Spatulata*. All these plants are easy to cultivate in the tropics and are shipped around the world from Southeast Asia in a multi-million dollar cut-flower industry. If living in a warm temperate climate, try growing *D. biggibum* 'compactum', a smaller, free-flowering plant from Queensland. Many succeed with it outdoors in sub-tropical climates such as Florida.

Section *Spatulata*

These used to be known as ceratobiums. A feature is the twisted sepals, which often go straight up, giving the section the popular name of "antelope orchids". The flowers are usually long-lasting. Most of the species come from low elevations or sea level and are definitely warm growers, needing a minimum night temperature of 60°C (15°C). Plenty of light and a warm humid atmosphere are beneficial. A medium as for cattleyas is suitable, but keep them growing throughout the year in small pots with frequent wet and dry cycles. Tall canes are typical, with leaves confined to the upper half. Flower stems carrying several flowers arise from the nodes of upper leaves. A few representative species are listed below.

Dendrobium canaliculatum. Found in Australia and Papua New Guinea growing on melaleuca trees. Flower stems carry 50 or more 1 in (2.5 cm) fragrant flowers in winter and spring. The flowers have white and yellow petals and sepals with a purple lip. Keep drier in winter than others in this section. It is a smaller plant than other spatulatas and has been much used in hybridization.

Dendrobium gouldii. A common species found growing over a wide geographic area. Flowers are 2¼ in (6 cm) across in white or pale violet with rarer golden yellow forms. Also widely used in hybridization.

Dendrobium stratiotes. This is a majestic species with 39 in (1 m) high canes and large, long-lasting flowers with white petals, yellow sepals and a violet lip. Flowers throughout the year.

Dendrobium tangerinum. The 3 in (7.5 cm) flowers have bright orange petals and yellow sepals and lip. This colorful plant was grown for many years under the name 'Tangerine'. It has been the parent of many hybrids.

Dendrobium Bellinger River

CHAPTER 13

The Oncidium Alliance

The plants in this chapter belong to a sub-tribe known as the Oncidiinae. They grow naturally in the tropical and sub-tropical Americas and the Caribbean, mainly as epiphytes. There are a confusing number of genera and hundreds of species. Some sections interbreed freely in cultivation and there are a large number of intergeneric names. The taxonomists have recently had a field day with this sub-tribe and many plants we know as odonto-glossums and oncidiums have been reclassified and given new names. Do not be too concerned if your plant label uses the species under the old genus name, as many of these have been retained, such as the Sander's hybrid list.

Central American odontoglossums

All the species below used to be classified under the genus name *Odontoglossum*. But pity we orchid growers who have just become accustomed to the genus *Lemboglossum*. It seems that the three lembo-glossums listed below, transferred from *Odonto-glossum* not so long ago, are to be transferred yet again, this time to the genus *Rhynchostele*. The plants grow in moist, cool, cloud forests. They will succeed under the same culture as Colombian odontoglossums (see pages 68-69) but seem to tolerate greater extremes of light and temperature (from 46°F-80°F/8°C-26°C, or higher, with good air movement).

Lemboglossum bictoniense. A plant that can grow 39 in (1 m) high with tall, erect spikes bearing 20 or so long-lasting 1¹/₂ in (4 cm) flowers opening in succession. The sepals and petals are brownish with a striking white or pink lip. It flowers in late summer. *L. uro-skinneri* is a similar, and perhaps prettier, species.

Miltoniopsis Maufant 'Jersey'

Lemboglossum cervantesii. This is a small plant producing up to six relatively large 2 in (5 cm) flowers in early spring that are white with unusual, reddish-brown, concentric rings near the center of the sepals and petals.

Lemboglossum rossii. Similar to *L. cervantesii*, but the flowers are somewhat larger and variable in color. Both are popular species.

Cuitlauzina pendula. This used to be called either *Odontoglossum pendulum* or *O. citrosmum*. It has glossy green pseudobulbs and deep green leaves. The flower stem emerges in spring from a new vegetative growth when this growth is only about 2 in (5 cm) high. The flower stem makes surprisingly rapid growth and becomes long and pendulous. There are many white or pink, fragrant, 2 in (5 cm) flowers. The inflorescence has a compelling charm that is difficult to describe and plants are much sought after. The plant must be kept dry in winter. If the pseudobulbs have not shriveled a little at the time the new vegetative growth appears in the spring, it has been watered too often and is unlikely to flower. Resume normal watering only after the flower stem appears.

Below: *Odontioda* Saint Aubins Bay 'Dresden'

Osmoglossum pulchellum. Leaves are stiff and grass-like and the flower stem has up to 10 pretty white flowers about 1 in (2.5 cm) in diameter in spring. Some grow the plant for its exceptionally strong and delightful fragrance.

Colombian odontoglossums

These are species which grow as epiphytes in the high Andes at elevations of up to 10,000 ft (3000 m). There are several species, mostly with yellow or white flowers blotched with brown, purple or red but, with one or possibly two exceptions, few are seen in cultivation now. The most famous is *Odontoglossum crispum*. This was found with flowers in a variety of color forms but almost all those now in cultivation have relatively massive, pure white flowers, the result of over 80 years of line breeding initiated in England. Hybridized with some of the other species, *O. crispum* has given us a galaxy of colors and color combinations. The incorporation of *Cochlioda noezliana*, a species with small scarlet flowers, has given us the intergeneric hybrid

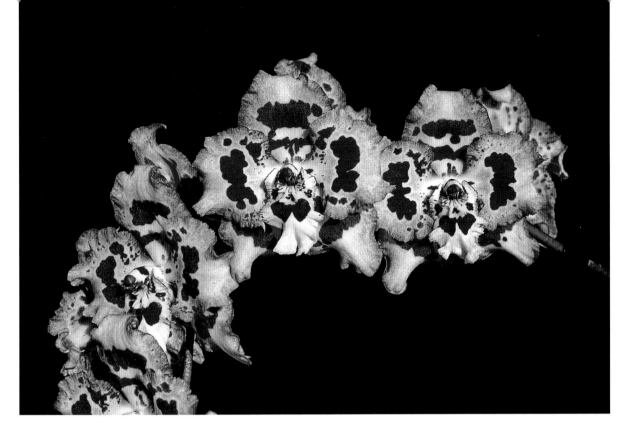

Odontioda Ispann

Odontioda, which can have solid red flowers in some cultivars.

A good, well-grown, modern *Odontoglossum* or *Odontioda* plant has leaves some 12 in (30 cm) in length and flat flowers up to 4 in (10 cm) across with as many as 20 to a stem. They are regarded as cool-growers, but although they will survive low temperatures short of freezing, the best-grown plants seem to

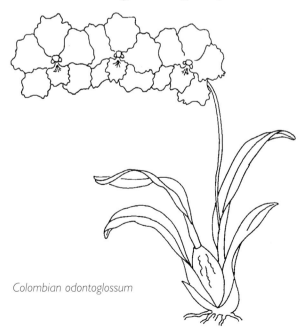

Colombian odontoglossum

come from a temperature regime that is neither too hot nor too cold. Nightly minimums of 50°F (10°C) are adequate. Maximum day temperatures of 68°F (20°C) are ideal. As high light is not needed, move the plant away from any windows or filter the light to ensure the temperature doesn't get too high. The plants will be cooler near the floor of a greenhouse in summer and can be heavily shaded. About 1500 foot-candles is adequate. These plants respond sensationally to regular or almost continuous misting or evaporative cooling on hot summer days.

Colombian odontoglossums in a shade-house will survive weeks of continuous cold, winter rain and a sodden growing medium without coming to any apparent harm or even loss of roots. However, they do not make much growth and flowering seems to be inhibited later in the season.

They are best not quite dried out between waterings in summer but should be allowed to dry in cold, dull, winter weather. A bark medium suits them and some growers have good results potting the plants in pure sphagnum moss, and keeping them damp year-round.

Flowers can come at any time of the year. Plants blooming in hot summer weather usually have quite poor flower quality. Some growers pinch out any new flower stems then to encourage flowers in a cooler season. Odontoglossums will be difficult to grow well without artificial cooling if subjected to long periods of temperatures above 90°F (32°C).

Miltoniopsis

This is the name now given to the so-called Colombian miltonias, although they are found elsewhere. They are still treated as the genus *Miltonia* in naming intergeneric hybrids with other genera, and are often referred to as "pansy orchids", due to the general appearance of the flowers. One to several flowers open on a stem in colors ranging from white or yellow to deep purple, often with a central pattern of a different color, called a mask. The plants have oval, compressed pseudobulbs and 8 in (20 cm), fragile-looking, gray-green leaves. Hybrids seem to be grown most often these days but occasionally seen are two of the important ancestral species, *Miltoniopsis vexillaria* and *Miltoniopsis roezlii*.

Miltoniopsis are high-elevation plants from wet cloud forests. Light intensity, temperatures and potting media are the same as for *Odontoglossum*. Do not over-pot, water before the medium has quite dried out in summer but let it dry out (but not for long) in winter.

Having said this, it is noticeable that growers with the most superbly grown and flowered plants usually keep their nightly minimum temperatures between 54°F (12°C) and 60°F (15°C). These plants are ideal for growing on window sills and in the company of *Phalaenopsis*. The flowering season is spring and summer.

Miltonia

These are referred to as Brazilian miltonias, a term often used to distinguish them from *Miltoniopsis* when both were called miltonias. The flowers are more star-shaped and with a less generous lip than their Colombian cousins.

This genus has been extensively used with other members of the oncidium alliance to produce many

Miltoniopsis

widely grown intergeneric hybrids. A species still very popular in cultivation is *Miltonia spectabilis*, with flattened pseudobulbs and 6 in (15 cm) yellowish-green foliage. The somewhat flattened flower stems bear one or two 3 in (7.5 cm) flowers in summer. Variety *moreliana* has large, deep-purple flowers and is widely cultivated. Brazilian miltonias have a reputation of being easy to grow. They are more tolerant of less-than-perfect conditions than the Colombian miltoniopsis. They will grow with, and can be treated the same as, cattleyas.

Oncidium

There are probably over 500 species in this genus widely spread over the Americas' tropics and subtropics. With so many species growing under varied conditions, it is not possible to give specific advice about requirements in cultivation that will apply to all. If in doubt, treat them as one would cattleyas, allowing them to dry out between waterings. A 46°F (8°C) minimum will suit cool-growers but 60°F (15°C) is best where higher temperatures are recommended. The species below are themselves common in collections. Also included below are the genera *Cyrtochilum*, *Psychopsis* and *Tolumnia* that we used to know as oncidiums. Although they have been transferred to other genera in recent times, they seem best dealt with in this section. Practically all are epiphytes.

Oncidium crispum. A cool-grower from Brazil that will tolerate lower temperatures than most other oncidiums. It has long rhizomes and long, wandering roots. Difficult, but not impossible to keep in a pot, it does well on a large slab. The inflorescence is branched and can carry many handsome 3 in (8 cm) flowers of a glossy chestnut color. Not to be confused with *Odontoglossum crispum*. Similar species of smaller plants include *Oncidium forbesii* and *Oncidium sarcodes*.

Oncidium luridum. This is a large plant with thick, rigid leaves. The branched inflorescence can be well over 39 in (1 m) long, carrying many $1^{1}/_{4}$ in (3 cm) yellow and reddish-brown flowers. *Oncidium cavendishianum*, *Oncidium lanceanum* and *Oncidium carthagenense* are similar plants and are referred to as "mule ear orchids". They prefer higher night temperatures and higher light levels than other oncidiums. Water with caution when not in active growth. These orchids are spring- and summer-flowering.

Cyrtochilum macranthum

Oncidium

Oncidium varicosum. The sepals and petals are relatively small, the dominant feature being the $1^{1}/_{2}$ in (4 cm) or wider pure yellow lip. Long, branched stems can carry as many as 100 flowers, or even more on a strong plant. A gentle breeze will move the flowers in a fanciful floral ballet, hence the common name for this and similar species of "dancing doll orchid". Mostly seen in cultivation is the superior variety *O. varicosum* var *rogersii*, which flowers in fall through to spring. It is often used to make hybrids where its shape and color is dominant even into the second generation. It is also very tolerant of temperature variations.

Cyrtochilum macranthum. Some authorities think this one should be left in genus *Oncidium*. The heavily substanced, bright yellow flowers are 3 in (8 cm) or more across. They are borne on a very long (typically a 39 in/1 m) branching stem that has a climbing tendency, winding its way around a support. A large plant in flower is an impressive sight. This is a cool-grower from the high Andes that flowers in spring or summer.

Psychopsis papilio. Found in tropical South America and the Caribbean, this orchid, as its name implies, is commonly called the "butterfly orchid". It does not require imagination to see how these large yellow and brown flowers mimic a large insect. They are, nevertheless, pretty flowers that open in succession from a tall spike at any season. The leaves are green and decoratively mottled with red-brown. The plants can be grown as and with cattleyas but prefer somewhat higher minimum temperatures at night.

Psychopsis kramerianum is a similar species. Do not remove flower stems after a plant has flowered as these old stems may produce more flowers some months later.

Tolumnia variegata. Native to the Caribbean, this orchid is one of a group of species often known as the "equitant oncidiums" or the "variegata oncidiums" because the plants are all similar in appearance to this species. *T. variegata* is a small orchid, native to Florida and some islands in the Caribbean, and is usually found growing in dry scrub or woods or on fence posts. The leaves are fleshy with a sharp end point and there is little in the way of a pseudobulb. The branched flower stem can be up to 16 in (40 cm) in length with many long-lasting flowers in pink and orangey brown. A galaxy of hybrids exists which flower year-round in a rainbow of colors, many with bright, complicated color patterns.

   Tolumnias thrive in minimum night temperatures of 55°F (12°C) and good light – at least as much as cymbidiums. The secret to successful culture is to dry the roots out very quickly after watering. The safest way to grow them is to mount the plants on slabs, cork slabs being particularly suitable. If pots must be used, choose clay rather than plastic. These plants have been successfully grown in empty clay pots.

Mule ear oncidium

Equitant oncidium

Other genera
Brassia. These are often called "spider orchids" due to the very long, thin petals and sepals. *Brassia verrucosa* is often cultivated. This is a fairly large plant some 32 in (80 cm) high. The flowers are mainly combinations of green, brown and white, with up to a dozen borne on a long stem. The thin sepals can be 4 in (10 cm) long. *B. gireoudiana* and *B. maculata* are among the other species cultivated. They are not difficult to grow if treated in all respects like cattleyas, but perhaps with a little more shade. There are a great many hybrids among other genera, particularly with *Miltonia*, *Oncidium* and *Odontoglossum*.

Comparettia. These are dwarfish plants with leathery leaves and little in the way of pseudobulbs. They can be grown in small pots, but do better on a slab. Comparettias do not like high light intensities, needing much the same growing environment as Colombian miltoniopsis. They bear up to 20 or so 2 in (5 cm) or smaller showy flowers on a stem, the large lip being a prominent feature. *Comparettia coccinea* has red flowers; C. *falcata* has cerise flowers and C. *speciosa* has striking orange flowers.

Rodriguezia. A genus of over 30 species growing up to 5000 ft (1500 m) in wet cloud forests throughout the tropical Americas. Popular in collections is the pretty species *Rodriguezia secunda*, a plant about 8 in (20 cm) high with leathery leaves that can produce several flower stems from the same growth, mainly in summer but occasionally at other times. The rose or red flowers are $1^{1}/_{4}$ in (3 cm) across. These plants can be grown the same way as cattleyas, but may need a little more shade. They do best mounted on a slab. Otherwise keep them in a clay pot that is not too large.

Cochlioda noezliana

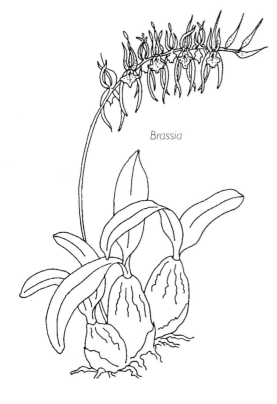

Brassia

Comparettia

CHAPTER 14

Paphiopedilum and Phragmipedium

The genera *Cypripedium*, *Paphiopedilum*, *Phragmipedium* and *Selenipedium* have a similar flower structure, where the lip is in the form of a pouch or a slipper and they are all referred to as "slipper orchids". There are two anthers with pollinia instead of one and a shield-like structure called the "staminode" protecting the reproductive parts. The dorsal sepal is relatively large and the two lateral sepals are joined together and called a "synsepal".

Cypripediums are terrestrial orchids and are widely distributed in northern temperate Asia, Europe, Japan and North America. They are not easy to bring into cultivation and are best left to grow where they are unless threatened in some way. Selenipediums are native from Costa Rica south to tropical South America. They are often tall plants, some up to 13 ft (4 m). They are rarely seen in cultivation and neither these nor cypripediums will be discussed further. Paphiopedilums have always been popular orchids and phragmipediums have become widespread in cultivation in recent years.

Paphiopedilums

The genus comprises some 60 species and are found growing in much the same geographical area as dendrobiums, though not as far south as Australia. In horticulture, paphiopedilums were once called cypripediums. In nature many, but not all, grow in low light in the organic litter on the forest floor or sometimes in the crevices in rocks. A few species are epiphytes. The plants are fan-shaped with leathery leaves and no pseudobulb. The flower stem arises terminally. The flowering season for most species is

Opposite: *Paphiopedilum callosum*, the colored form of the species.

Paphiopedilum Goultenianum 'La Tuilere', a 'Maudiae type' hybrid.

winter to spring but there are some exceptions. Not too long ago the main interest of orchid growers was in what are sometimes called exhibition hybrids. These are the result of 100 years of breeding, which has given us massive flowers with a wide dorsal sepal, wide, flat petals and generous lips or pouches in colors of brown, purple, yellow, green, white and near-red. In recent years a lot of interest has been

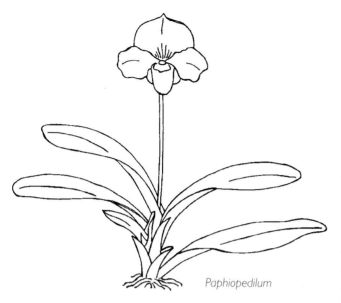

Paphiopedilum

moved to species and primary hybrids. This has been fueled by the discovery and introduction of many new species.

Culture
Temperature
Plants with mottled leaves tend to come from warmer climates and need higher minimum temperatures. Those with plain green leaves will usually tolerate lower temperatures, but there are exceptions. Species with multiple flowers have green leaves but are warmer-growing. For these the usually recommended minimum night temperature is 60°F (15°C). Minimums of 50°F (10°C), or occasionally even lower, are appropriate for cooler growers. Many kinds fit somewhere between these figures. Some paphiopedilums must have a nightly drop in temperature to below 60°F (15°C) for several weeks from early fall to initiate flowering.

Light
Most paphiopedilums do not require high light intensities, and can be grown in an east or west window, or near a shaded south window. Under artifical light, they require between 1000 and 2000 foot-candles. Too little light will inhibit flowering.

Too much light reduces the plant size, number of leaves, flower quality and stem length.

Watering and nutrition
The plants should not be allowed to become bone dry at the roots. Water when the growing medium is still just moist but not wet. If in doubt during the summer, water, but if in doubt in winter, don't. Include nutrients in the water at the same strength recommended for epiphytes. Slow-release fertilizers may be used but it would be safer to keep them on the surface.

Potting
All kinds of recipes have been tried, but these days paphiopedilums are nearly always seen in bark-based mixes. Some species grow in limestone country and the addition of lime to the mix is supposed to be beneficial. Add dolomite lime to bark-based media in the quantities suggested in Chapter 5. Paphiopedilums are less resentful about being removed from their pots than are other orchids, but they are best left two years in the same container. Try not to damage the brittle roots. Do not over-pot and do not bury the plant below the surface of the medium. The rhizome should not be deeper than $1/4$ in (5 mm) below the surface of the medium. Re-potted plants may need staking until they get established. The best time to re-pot is after flowering.

Pests and diseases
Paphiopedilums are susceptible to foliage rots caused by fungi and bacteria. Static water is the basic cause of these problems. At all costs avoid leaving water to lie in leaf axils, particularly in the developing growth. Rot here can quickly develop to the point where it is difficult to save the plant. Be especially careful when watering. Treat problems as suggested in Chapter 7 and if they persist spray regularly with a preventative fungicide in an attempt to remedy the source of the trouble. Pests are not too

Opposite: *Phragmipedium* Memoria Dick Clement 'Condor'. The red color comes from one parent, *Phrag. besseae*.

troublesome but watch out particularly for scale and mealybug.

Propagation

Large plants are best divided into smaller divisions. Ensure that each division has some active roots. Try cutting the rhizomes, but delay their removal from their pot for a few months to give the divisions a chance to make new roots and growths before being disturbed. Attempts to tissue-culture paphiopedilums have not been successful and, for this reason, particularly choice cultivars are difficult and expensive to obtain.

Fortunately, paphiopedilums can be raised from seed. The most rewarding way to add to your collection is to purchase unflowered seedlings. Some of them do not make particularly rapid growth, but small plants will reach flowering size more quickly if they are given somewhat higher minimum temperatures than adult plants. Some successful growers advocate putting deflasked seedlings in a pot from which a healthy adult plant has just been removed or incorporating a little of the growing medium from that pot in another container with the seedlings.

Housing

In climate Zone 10 or favorable areas in climate Zone 9, the cooler-growing species such as *Paphiopedilum insigne* can be grown in a shade-house. Otherwise this genus needs to be grown indoors or in a greenhouse. Many are suitable indoor subjects and good plants are often seen growing on window sills. In this situation be careful to ensure that the plants are not exposed to full sun.

Phragmipediums

The genus is related to paphiopedilums but occupies an entirely separate geographical distribution, being

Paphiopedilum fairrieanum 'Red Top'

native to the tropical Americas. Most of the species have flowers in shades of green and brown but there are colorful exceptions. The dorsal sepal often has a shape similar to the petals but the latter are often greatly elongated and drooping – up to 39 in (1 m) in *Phragmipedium cordatum*.

Water is important in the culture of this genus. The more frequent the watering in summer the better, and never let the medium approach dryness even in winter. Many species are bog plants and enjoy water continuously flowing past their roots. A modern cultural practice is to stand the pots in a tray of water about $1/2$ in or less (1 cm) deep, but the water must be changed daily or, better still, have it flowing continuously past the roots. Under these conditions the roots will often go down into the water through the drainage holes in the pot.

Other than watering, phragmipediums may be grown in a similar way to paphiopedilums. However, having so much water around leaves the plant

susceptible to fungal and bacterial attack, especially in winter. Be careful not to leave water lying on the stems and leaves for any length of time. Phragmipediums are acid-loving plants and it has been recommended that you do not incorporate any lime into the potting medium. The plants are best re-potted into fresh potting medium each year after flowering. Temperature minimums of 54°F-60°F (12°C-15°C) are desirable, even for species described as cooler growers.

Paphiopedilum armeniacum. The discovery of this species in China and its introduction to cultivation in the 1980s, generated much excitement – nobody had seen this color in paphiopedilums before. The better forms bear roundish 3 in (8 cm) flowers of an all-over, deep yellow color with gold overtones. A cool-grower.

Paphiopedilum callosum. A vigorous grower that has pale green leaves with some mottling. The green and white flowers are marked with vertical purple lines. Some varieties are dark purple while others are white and green. One of the progenitors of the so-called "maudiae-type" paphiopedilums.

Paphiopedilum fairriaeanum. The dorsal sepals have a white base with dark purple longitudinal veins. Combination white-green forms are common. The downswept petals with upturned tips give this species its characteristic appearance. This is a smallish plant with green leaves from the foothills of the Himalayas, and is usually regarded as a cool-grower.

Paphiopedilum glaucophyllum. This is a tall plant, up to 20 in (50 cm) high. The flower stem bears several flowers that open sequentially one at a time as each old flower dies. The plant can remain in flower for several months. The dorsal sepal is green, brown and white and the lip is pink. It may need warmer temperatures than the other species.

Paphiopedilum insigne. In years past this Himalayan species was one of the most common paphioped-

Paphiopedilum Captain Cook 'Discovery'

ilums seen in homes and greenhouses. It is in the ancestry of most modern, complex, so-called exhibition hybrids. The flower color is very variable, but typically has a green dorsal sepal with brown spots and a white edging, with the petals and lip brownish. The shape of the flower is less than perfect compared with modern hybrids. However, it is a cool-growing species and a good, easy-to-grow beginner's orchid. In winter the pots may be allowed to approach dryness before the next watering.

Paphiopedilum micranthum. Another species with dark, mottled leaves found in southwestern China at elevations over 3300 ft (1000 m). It has a large pink pouch or lip, the other floral segments being green striped with purple. The flowers can be over 3 in (8 cm) in width.

Paphiopedilum rothschildianum. A much sought-after plant found growing on Mt. Kinabalu in Borneo, where it is now rare due to over-collection. There are three or more distinctive flowers on a tall stem. The

dorsal sepal is greenish white with bold, vertical, brownish stripes. The lip is cinnamon. The petals are narrow, elongated and held horizontally. This species has plain green leaves but is a warm-grower and needs brighter light than most paphiopedilums.

Phragmipedium besseae. It is hard to believe that this species with its flat, well-proportioned, vibrant red flowers on tall stems escaped notice until it was described, as recently as 1981, as coming from Peru. It has since been found farther afield and there are now a number of varieties, including a yellow form. The introduction of the species into cultivation helped to trigger the current resurgence of interest in this genus.

Phragmipedium longifolium. A plant with 24 in (10 cm) long leaves and a flower stem over 39 in (1 m) high with several flowers that open one at a time. The flowers are pale yellowish-green with twisted 4 in (10 cm) pendulous red-brown flowers.

CHAPTER 15

Phalaenopsis

Phalaenopsis, the moth orchid, comprises some 40 to 50 species native to a wide tropical area in India, Southeast Asia, Indonesia, the Philippines and northern Australia. They are mainly epiphytes, although some can grow as lithophytes. The genus is characterized by fleshy, wandering roots and succulent leaves. A flower stem can carry anything from a few flowers to up to 100 on a branched stem. The flowers are flat and of heavy substance, in many colors and a diversity of patterns. Flowers are typically about 3 in (7.5 cm) across but many are smaller and some modern hybrids can reach well over 4 in (10 cm) in size.

The genus is now widely cultivated by hobbyist growers and commercial growers produce them for the cut-flower trade. A collection of flowering plants is a breathtaking sight. The long-lasting flowers stand up well to packing and transportation and are popular with florists. Flowers are mostly seen in winter and spring, but even a modest collection can have plants in flower in all seasons. The genus is monopodial with no pseudobulbs, new leaves appearing one on top of the other during the life of the plant. If the growing point is destroyed, a lower node on the stem may break into a new vegetative growth. The flower stem emerges from inside one of the upper leaves.

In nature the flower stems are mostly pendulous, but in cultivation it is more convenient to stake them in a semi-arching position. If, when removing flowers, the stem is severed just below the bottom flower, a node lower than this may produce more

Opposite: *Phalaenopsis* Cinnamon Sugar 'Primo' Top right: *Phalaenopsis* Snow Leopard

blooms. However, they will probably be smaller on this secondary stem and this only happens on a well-established plant.

Culture
Phalaenopsis are tropical plants and failures are often experienced by growers who do not provide the warm temperatures they need. On the other hand, if temperatures are to their liking, the plants can be quite forgiving grown in otherwise less-than-perfect conditions.

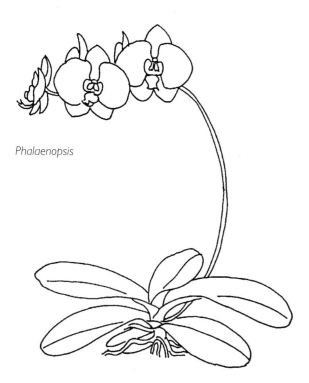

Phalaenopsis

Housing

Other genera needing different light intensities and temperatures are best not kept in the company of *Phalaenopsis* as it is difficult to grow them all well. *Phalaenopsis* can be successfully grown inside your house if it is kept reasonably warm. Proper shading must be provided on a window sill. Placing the plant over (but not in) a tray containing water might provide a little extra humidity in the area of the plant. The relative humidity indoors can be a little too low for comfort, but frequent misting will help. If growing in a greenhouse, it is often possible to enclose a section with plastic sheeting to create an area where the correct environment for a small collection can be provided.

Temperature

The ideal night minimum is probably about 68°F (20°C) and young seedlings will make the best growth in this environment. In nature, many species enjoy warmer night temperatures than this. However, in cultivation adult plants can be grown quite well with minimums of 60°F (15°C). A very occa-

sional fall to 50°F (10°C) will do no damage. In fact a drop down to 55°F (13°C) for two to four weeks will help to initiate flowering with some kinds. Do not overdo it. Young leaves have been damaged when exposed to 44°F (7°C) for more than four hours. Warm daytime temperatures up to 95°F (35°C) can be tolerated, especially if humidity is not too low and the leaves do not get hot.

Light

In nature most species grow in the shade of the forest canopy. Place in an east, west or shaded south window and protect from direct sun. In a greenhouse give them about the same amount or a little less than paphiopedilums enjoy. About 1000 to 1500 foot-candles is correct. Too much light gives stunted, yellowish plants and too little, soft, fleshy, dark green plants, which may not flower.

Humidity

Relative humidities of over 70 percent but less than 100 percent are the ideal but are not easy to achieve on a hot summer's day. Some suggestions for maintaining humidity are in Chapter 2. In the greenhouse, misters with the water directed under benches but not on the plants are effective and popular.

Potting

The roots have a tendency to wander outside the pot and resent efforts to coax them back. These aerial roots are best left that way. Bark is now the most used potting material either on its own or mixed with pieces of polystyrene, charcoal, pumice, sphagnum moss and other materials.

Mature plants usually need the potting medium replaced every two years. If they can continue to be accommodated in the same pot do not attempt to remove the plant from the pot and thus damage the roots. Knock out the old medium and work fresh material in and around the roots in the pot. If a larger pot is essential, try to damage the roots as little as possible. If in a clay pot (the best for beginners), sacrifice the pot by breaking it into

Phalaenopsis (lindenii × aphrodite)

pieces with a hammer so that the pieces with roots adhering can also be moved into the new pot. Probably the best way to grow *Phalaenopsis* is in a basket. A plastic net can be used to stop the bark medium from falling out.

Watering and nutrition
Do not let the medium quite dry out between waterings. Try to get the aerial roots to take in some water. To this end they can be sprayed or drenched frequently with water during the daytime. Use soluble nutrients at the 100 ppm N strength as covered in Chapter 6. Do not water with ice-cold water as this can cause leaf damage.

Pests and diseases
Phalaenopsis can be attacked by most of the pests that infest other orchids. Watch out for tiny mites (you will need a magnifying glass) that can cause silvering on either leaf surface. Any leaf rot should be cut out immediately and a protective fungicide applied. This particularly applies to the crown of the plant, even if the developing growth is destroyed entirely. The plant is not necessarily then doomed, as new growths may eventually develop from the base. Water or moisture allowed to lie too long on the leaves is the cause of this trouble, as it enables disease agents to gain a foothold. Try swabbing areas affected with black rot with one of the quarternary ammonium compounds mentioned in Chapter 7. Do it both before and after cutting out the rot.

Propagation
The flower stems will sometimes produce keikis or plantlets from nodes. These can be removed and potted as soon as they develop roots. The growth substance benzyl adenine (BA) will encourage this if applied to dormant buds on older flower stems.

Unflowered seedlings are available from commercial growers and there is usually a large selection of crosses. These can be very rewarding. The more vigorous seedlings out of a flask can flower in two or three years.

Phalaenopsis Kenneth Wong

Species and hybrids

Hybridization has given us a wide range of plants with flower quality and color combinations not seen in nature. There are intergeneric hybrids, the most common one being *Doritaenopsis* (*Doritis* x *Phalaenopsis*). A few species are still grown for their intrinsic beauty. The three below are often kept in collections.

Phalaenopsis amabilis. This species is found in the parentage of most modern hybrids, and the modern tetraploid hybrids with their massive white flowers are largely founded upon it. In the species, many stark white flowers up to 4 in (10 cm) in diameter are borne in profusion on long, branching stems. In nature, *P. amabilis* grows over a very large geographical range, as far south as northern Queensland in Australia. In cultivation it is tolerant of and may need higher light levels than other species.

Phalaenopsis equestris. A relatively small, compact plant with a zigzag flower stem bearing many 1 in (2.5 cm) flowers variable in color but commonly pale rose. It is native to the Philippines and Taiwan. The abundance of flowers on a compact plant has led to the breeding of a range of popular hybrids that grow in small pots and are sometimes referred to as "miniatures".

Phalaenopsis violacea. A summer-flowering species bearing a few 3 in (7.5 cm) fragrant flowers that open one or two at a time in succession. Flower size and color is variable, including white forms. The variety from Malaysia has star-shaped, smaller, mainly pinkish flowers. The variety from Borneo has larger flowers in a typical form, with greenish sepals and petals with a deep violet-purple center – the latter color probably being responsible for the popularity of the species. *P. violacea* needs more shade than most other species.

CHAPTER 16

Other Orchids

Space does not permit a discussion of every kind of orchid. However, together with those already covered, the following would probably include the majority of the different genera in cultivation.

Ascocentrum. The genus is related to *Vanda*, which it resembles in habit but is smaller. Ascocentrum species have showy flowers and are widely cultivated. *A. curvifolium* has an upright stem densely packed with 1 in (2.5 cm) red to orange flowers in late spring and summer. *A. miniatum* is a smaller plant with bright flowers from yellow and orange to vermillion red. Most plants with this label may really be *A. garayi*. Culture is the same as *Vanda*, with a minimum temperature of 55°F (12°C).

Catasetum. A genus of over 70 species, mainly epiphytic, found in the Central and South American tropics. They mostly have thick, stocky pseudobulbs and tend to be deciduous. The flowers are male and female. Usually all the flowers on a stem are either all male or all female, but occasionally both appear on the same stem. There is a large color range, with green dominant in most, but not all, species. The male flower is typically the most colorful. The female is usually green. Catasetums can be grown in bark and cultivated like cattleyas, although they prefer a little more warmth and light when in active growth. (Min. temp. of 50°F/10°C when resting as opposed to 64°F/18°C when growing.) Much higher light intensities encourage the production of female flowers. Water carefully when the new vegetative shoot is developing as it is prone to rot. Water well when the new growth is nearing maturity and sparingly after the leaves are shed.

Ascocentrum miniatum

This genus has one feature that makes it a great conversation piece. The male flowers of many species will shoot out pollinia with great force if sensitive antennae at the base of the column are touched. A pollinating bee is the target but the flower will spit the pollen at you, too, if you touch it.

Coelogyne. These are sympodial plants with pseudobulbs. Some species have long rhizomes and are best grown in a basket. The flower stems

Disa watsonii

often emerge from the center of new growths. In the main, they like somewhat brighter light than cattleyas. India, China, Indonesia and some Pacific islands are where they grow naturally. *C. cristata* is a cool-grower from higher altitudes in the Himalayan foothills and has attractive, pure white, up to 4 in (10 cm) wide flowers in spring. It can be grown in a shade-house all year, if unlikely to be frozen, or on a windowsill and is considered a good plant for beginners in cooler climates. *C. pandurata* has emerald-green flowers with a striking black-marked lip that attracts immediate attention. This one is a warmer-grower needing night minimums of around 60°F (15°C).

Disa. About 130 species are distributed throughout Africa. Only half a dozen, all terrestrial plants from the south of the continent, are in cultivation. The flowers are in colors of red, pink, yellow and even blue. Attractive hybrids are being raised from these species. The flowers have prominent sepals, a large erect dorsal and rather insignificant petals and lips in most species. Interest in this genus is increasing. Florists have been introduced to them and they are now being grown for cut flowers. The best known of the disas is *Disa uniflora* (sometimes *grandiflora*) known as the "Pride of Table Mountain". This one has large 4 in (10 cm) wide flowers, one or two to a stem, and the common variety is a brilliant scarlet.

The potting medium most popular is either pure sphagnum moss or a peat-based mix, but with a lower proportion of peat than contained in the mix in Chapter 5. Do not add lime as disas need a medium on the acidic side. The pot must drain well but must not be allowed to become dry at any time. In nature, plants often grow in wet stream-side habitats. Disas respond to good-quality water. A modern practice is to have the bottom 1 in (2.5 cm) or a little more of the pot permanently submerged in water. The water must be kept fresh. Ideally the water should be circulating through the container all the time – the inlet at one end and the drain at the other. Warm air temperatures are no problem if the roots are kept cool, nor are low temperatures down to near-freezing in winter. Place in an east- or south-facing position, but protect from direct sunlight. They can be grown year-round in a shade-house under 50 percent shade-cloth with overhead protection from rain but they cannot survive being frozen. In a greenhouse up to 4000 foot-candles is appropriate. The winter minimum temperature is controversial, but may be as low as 46°F (8°C).

After blooming in summer, the flowering growth dies but there will be an emerging new growth that will develop and flower the following summer. Re-potting is best done in fall after flowering. It is possible to raise seedlings by sowing the seed on sphagnum moss, or sterilized peat, or otherwise employing techniques used for begonias and ferns. This does not always work and disas are raised commercially by flasking.

Lycaste. A sympodial epiphytic or occasionally lithophytic genus growing naturally from Mexico to

Disa Unifoam

Peru. The flowers have relatively large sepals and somewhat smaller petals, which in most species tend to come forward over the column. Yellow, yellow-green and green are common colors but there are pink species. Many are deciduous, dropping all their leaves in winter and flowering in the spring from leafless pseudobulbs. The plants need moisture, nutrients and warmth when in full growth but must be kept drier in winter, especially the deciduous kinds. Light intensities should be about the same as for cattleyas or a little less, but, if growing under lights, not more than 2000 foot-candles in summer. Bark is the widely used potting medium but some growers get better results with a heavier mix, often peat-based. Minimum temperatures of 50°F (10°C) or a little warmer are suitable. The queen of the lycastes and probably the most common in cultivation is *Lycaste skinneri*, the national flower of Guatemala. It is sometimes known as *L. virginalis*. The pink flowers, in spring, are of heavy substance and have been seen up to

Lycaste

Masdevallia

Masdevallia Minaret 'L & R'

6 in (15 cm) in diameter, though they are usually smaller. There is also a pure white form and some hybrids with other species.

Masdevallia. A bewildering number of species exist, perhaps 400 or more, and more new ones are frequently being discovered and described. They are found throughout the tropical Americas, but most grow as epiphytes in the high Andes of Colombia, Ecuador and Peru. There are no pseudobulbs and a single fleshy leaf grows from the rhizome. These are all relatively small plants. The flowers are very variable, with colors ranging from the brilliant to the somber and the overall appearance from the very beautiful to the bizarre. The most prominent feature of the flower, the sepals, are in many species greatly elongated to long tails. Fascination with these plants is attracting more and more growers worldwide.

Masdevallias like cool, shady, moist conditions. Minimum temperatures of 50°F (10°C) are often mentioned in literature but they can go a lot lower than this in their native habitat. These orchids can be grown indoors, in an unheated greenhouse with good air movement or in a shade-house with overhead rain protection, provided temperatures do not drop near freezing. Keeping the plants cool in summer is more of a problem, as they resent high temperatures, so move them away from windows in warm temperatures. An eastern window with no direct sunlight is ideal, or a light level of 1000 foot-candles, or a little more in winter. A bark-based potting mix can be used but just about everything has been tried. Never let the medium quite dry out. A few species have flower stems that grow straight down and need basket culture.

The genus *Dracula* is a relative with fascinating somber-colored flowers and needs the same growing conditions.

Sarcochilus. The sub-tribe Sarcanthinae is where this genus belongs, along with *Vanda*, *Phalaenopsis* and a number of other genera in cultivation. They are all monopodial in growth habit. *Sarcochilus* plants look like vandas but are much smaller. Most of the species grow as spring-flowering epiphytes or lithophytes east of the Great Dividing Range of Australia. Very popular is S. *hartmannii* which bears up to 16 flowers about 1 in (2.5 cm) across in good varieties and in a range of colors, mainly white with rose or red markings. This is an upright plant that likes to have most of its root system covered and can be grown in a pot with a bark-based medium. S. *fitzgeraldii* has similar flowers and grows on mossy rocks, in deep gullies, and in coastal brush forests. S. *falcatus* is an epiphyte of the rainforest and is a popular plant with white, orange blossom-scented flowers – known as the "Orange Blossom Orchid".

Like most of the Sarcanthinae, this genus tends to have a few wandering roots that do not like being confined to a pot. S. *falcatus* above, for this reason, is better grown on a slab or in a basket. Most species do not require high light levels. As to temperature, S. *hartmannii* grows up to 6500 ft (2000 m) above sea level and, providing it does not freeze, grows well year-round in a shade-house under 50 percent shade-cloth with protection from overhead rain in winter and spring. Roots in a pot should not approach dryness, more especially in summer, but plants on slabs and exposed roots on any plant must be watered frequently. In general, this genus is not difficult to grow and extensive hybridization, mostly in Australia, is producing attractive hybrids of considerable horticultural importance.

Vanda. These are large monopodial orchids growing naturally from India and China down to Australia and the Philippines. They can be grown in pots, but most of the roots will prefer to wander around outside the pot. Culture in baskets is preferable but they need to be suspended, as the roots tend to hang downwards. A suitable potting medium is large pieces of bark with perhaps the inclusion of lumps of charcoal, pumice or even polystyrene. In bright,

Sarcochilis Melody

sunny, warm weather vandas need plenty of water and frequent misting of exposed roots. In cool or dull winter weather water sparingly, although the exposed roots can be misted. Vandas need feeding – use nutrients of the strength recommended for cymbidiums.

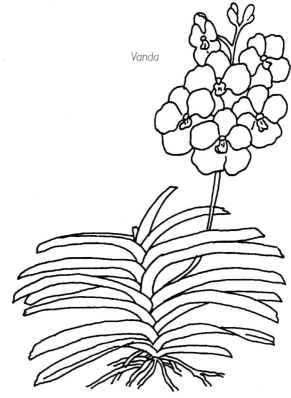

Vanda

For cultivation purposes vandas can be in one of two groups, terete and strap-leafed. Terete vandas, of which the species *Vanda teres* is typical, have leaves that are folded into a cylinder, giving them a thin, pencil-like appearance. A famous terete, believed to be a primary hybrid, is *V. Miss Joaquim*. This was named after the missionary in whose garden in Singapore the plant was found late in the 19th century. Terete vandas demand strong light for growth and flowering. In tropical areas, many are grown in full sun for cut flowers. They can be difficult subjects and you may wish to limit your collection of vandas to the strap-leafed kinds, or perhaps try semi-terete plants, which are hybrids between the two kinds.

Strap-leafed vandas also need strong light, but some shading is needed in summer. Temperatures should ideally not go below 55°F (12°C). Temperatures below 38°F (4°C) may cause damage to flower buds and root tips. *Vanda coerula* is much cooler-growing than all the other species and the best cultivars have deep sky-blue flowers, not a common color in orchids. This species and *V. sanderiana* (or *Euanthe sanderiana*) are in the ancestry of most modern hybrids. At various times these hybrids produce, from a node in the upper leaves, a stem of 10 or more round flowers at least 4 in (10 cm) in diameter in a large color range.

Vandas grow very tall in time. When they become too tall, cut off the top of the plant at a point where some roots have developed and it will make another plant. The original plant will usually make one or more new vegetative shoots in response to this. Often aerial growths develop on a vanda and these can be potted when they develop roots. Many intergeneric hybrids are grown. Very popular is *Ascocenda* (*Vanda* x *Ascocentrum*).

Zygopetalum. A sympodial genus from tropical South America. The plants are terrestrials or epiphytes and described as growing in wet forest at altitudes up to 5000 ft (1500 m). They are mostly spring-flowering and have pale green, glossy pseudobulbs and long, narrow leaves. Flower stems

Vanda propagation A. Sever the stem about where shown leaving at least four good roots on the top part. Note the sympodial growth habit.

Pot normally.

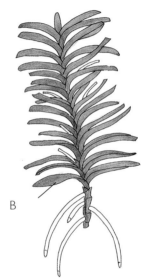

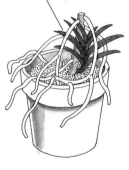

New growths initiated by severing top.

Vanda propagation B. The top portion can be established in a pot or raft. If left undisturbed the original plant should produce new shoots from near the base.

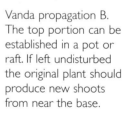

emerge from the base of the pseudobulbs and have 10 or more fragrant flowers up to 3¼ in (8.5 cm) in diameter. Flowers can be in rich colors of brown, green and violet. Very good hybrids are available including the colorful intergeneric *Propetalum* (*Zygopetalum* x *Promenaea*). Zygopetalums can be grown with cymbidiums and in the same potting mix.

Names of some cultivated intergeneric genera hybrids

ALICEARA *(Alcra.)*	BRASSIA x MILTONIA x ONCIDIUM
ASCOCENDA *(Ascda.)*	ASCOCENTRUM x VANDA
ASCOCENTRUM *(Asctm.)*	Natural genus
ASPASIA *(Asp.)*	Natural genus
ASPOGLOSSUM *(Aspgm.)*	ASPASIA x ODONTOGLOSSUM
BEALLARA *(Bllra.)*	BRASSIA x COCHLIODA x MILTONIA x ODONTOGLOSSUM
BRASSAVOLA *(B.)*	Natural genus
BRASSIA *(Brs.)*	Natural genus
BRASSIDIUM *(Brsdm.)*	BRASSIA x ONCIDIUM
BRASSOCATTLEYA *(Bc.)*	BRASSAVOLA x CATTLEYA
BRASSOLAELIOCATTLEYA *(Blc.)*	BRASSAVOLA x CATTLEYA x LAELIA
BROUGHTONIA *(Bro.)*	Natural genus
CATTLEYA *(C.)*	Natural genus
CATTLEYTONIA *(Ctna.)*	BROUGHTONIA x CATTLEYA
CHARLESWORTHARA *(Cha.)*	COCHLIODA x MILTONIA x ONCIDIUM
COCHLIODA *(Cda.)*	Natural genus
CYMBIDIUM *(Cym.)*	Natural genus
DENDROBIUM *(Den.)*	Natural genus
EPICATTLEYA *(Epc.)*	CATTLEYA x EPIDENDRUM
EPIDENDRUM *(Epi.)*	Natural genus
EPILAELIA *(Epil.)*	EPIDENDRUM x LAELIA
EPITONIA *(Eptn.)*	BROUGHTONIA x EPIDENDRUM
HAWKINSARA *(Hknsa.)*	BROUGHTONIA x LAELIA x CATTLEYA x SOPHRONITIS
HOWEARA *(Hwra.)*	LEOCHILIS x ONCIDIUM x RODRIGUESIA
LAELIA *(L.)*	Natural genus
LAELIOCATTLEYA *(Lc.)*	CATTLEYA x LAELIA
LOWARA *(Low.)*	BRASSAVOLA x LAELIA x SOPHRONITIS
LYCASTE *(Lyc.)*	Natural genus
MACLELLANARA *(Mclna.)*	BRASSIA x ODONTOGLOSSUM x ONCIDIUM
MASDEVALLIA *(Masd.)*	Natural genus
MILTASSIA *(Mtssa.)*	BRASSIA x MILTONIA
MILTONIA *(Milt.)*	Natural genus
MILTONIDIUM *(Mtdm.)*	MILTONIA x ONCIDIUM
ODONTIODA *(Oda.)*	COCHLIODA x ODONTOGLOSSUM
ODONTOBRASSIA *(Odbrs.)*	BRASSIA x ODONTOGLOSSUM
ODONTOCIDIUM *(Odcdm.)*	ODONTOGLOSSUM x ONCIDIUM
ODONTOGLOSSUM *(Odm.)*	Natural genus
ODONTONIA *(Odtna.)*	MILTONIA x ODONTOGLOSSUM
ONCIDIODA *(Oncda.)*	COCHLIODA x ONCIDIUM
ONCIDIUM *(Onc.)*	Natural genus
PAPHIOPEDILUM *(Paph.)*	Natural genus
PHALAENOPSIS *(Phal.)*	Natural genus
POTINARA *(Pot.)*	BRASSAVOLA x CATTLEYA x LAELIA x SOPHRONITIS
RHYNCHOSTYLIS *(Rhy.)*	Natural genus
RODRICIDIUM *(Rdcm.)*	ONCIDIUM x RODRIGUEZIA
RODRIGUEZIA *(Rdza.)*	Natural genus
SARTYLIS	SARCOCHILIS x RHYNCHOSTYLIS
SOPHROCATTLEYA *(Sc.)*	CATTLEYA x SOPHRONITIS
SOPHROLAELIA *(Sl.)*	LAELIA x SOPHRONITIS
SOPHROLAELIOCATTLEYA *(SlC.)*	CATTLEYA x LAELIA x SOPHRONITIS
SOPHRONITIS *(Soph.)*	Natural genus
VANDA *(V.)*	Natural genus
VUYLSTEKEARA *(Vuyl.)*	COCHLIODA x MILTONIA x ODONTOGLOSSUM
WILSONARA *(Wils.)*	COCHLIODA x ODONTOGLOSSUM x ONCIDIUM
ZYGOPETALUM *(Z.)*	Natural genus

Sources

Andy's Orchids, Inc.
734 Ocean View Avenue, Encinitas, CA 92024
U.S. Toll-Free Tel: 1-888-514-2639
U.S. Toll-Free Fax: 1-888-632-8991
Tel: (760) 436-4239 Fax: (760) 632-8991
Web: www.andysorchids.com
All species orchids, epiphytic and terrestrial.

Baker & Chantry, Inc.
PO Box 554, Woodinville, WA 98072
Tel: (425) 483-0345
Web: www.bakerandchantry.com
Miltoniopsis, paphiopedilum, stanhopea and lycaste.

Bloomfield Orchids
251 West Bloomfield Road, Pittsford, NY 14534
Tel: (716) 381-4206 Fax: (716) 383-5672
Email: bloomfld@frontiernet.net
Paphiopedilum and phragmipedium.

Brookside Orchid Garden
23779 32nd Avenue RR#12
Langley, BC V2Z 2J2
Tel: (604) 533-8286 Fax: (604) 533-0498
Web: www.brooksideorchids.com
Over 650 varieties of orchids.

Calwest Tropical Supply
11614 Sterling Avenue, Riverside, CA 92503
Toll-Free Tel: 1-800-301-9009
Tel: (909) 351-1880 Fax: (909) 351-1872
Supplies including New Zealand sphagnum moss.

Carter and Holmes Orchids
PO Box 668, Newberry, SC 29108
Tel: (803) 276-0579 Fax: (803) 276-0588
Web: www.carterandholmes.com
Cattleyas, phalaenopsis, paphiopedilums and species.

Clargreen Gardens
814 Southdown Road, Mississauga, ON L5J 2Y4
Tel: (905) 822-0992 Fax: (905) 822-7282
Web: www.clargreen.com
Phalaenopsis, many orchid species and hybrids.

Cloud's Orchids
108 Birchcliff Avenue
Scarborough, ON M1N 3C7
Tel: (416) 699-8685
Web: home.ica.net/~birch/

Dyna-Gro
1065 Broadway, San Pablo, CA 94806
Toll-Free Tel: 1-800-396-2476
Tel: (510) 233-0254
Liquid fertilizer formula.

Fantasy Orchids, Inc.
830 W. Cherry Street, Louisville, CO 80027
Tel: (303) 666-5432 Fax: (303) 666-7730
Web: www.fantasyorchids.com

Fox Valley Orchids Ltd.
2N134 Addison Road, Villa Park, IL 60181
Tel: (630) 458-0636 Fax: (630) 458-1030
Web: www.foxvalleyorchids.com
*Paphiopedilum sanderianum, phragmipedium,
parvisepalum and paphiopedilum.*

Hoosier Orchid Company
8440 West 82nd Street, Indianapolis, IN 46278
Tel: (317) 291-6269 Fax: (317) 291-8949
Web: www.hoosierorchid.com
*Seed-grown species, angracoids, pleurothallids,
zygopetalum.*

Huronview Nurseries
6429 Brigden Road, RR 1
Bright's Grove, ON N0N 1C0
Tel: (519) 869-4689 Fax: (519) 869-8518
Email: jonathanc@wwdc.com
Over 3000 orchids, supplies.

J & B Orchids
PO Box 245323, Brooklyn, N.Y. 11224
Tel/Fax: (718) 996-1064
Web: www.jandborchids.com

J & L Orchids
20 Sherwood Road, Easton, CT 06612
Tel: (203) 261-3772 Fax: (203) 261-8730
Web: www.orchidmall.com/jlorchids
Miniatures, unusual species, masdevallia.

Jim's Orchid Supplies
4157 Lebanon Road, Fort Pierce, FL 34982
Tel: (561) 489-0859 Fax: (810) 314-4253
Web: www.jimssupplies.com
Supplies and "under lights" equipment.

Juno Beach Orchids
15703 69th Drive North
Palm Beach Gardens, FL 33418
Tel: (561) 748-1296 Fax: (561) 748-1059
Web: www.jborchids.com
Easy-to-grow, free-blooming orchids.

Kelley's Korner Orchid Supplies
PO Box 6, Kittery, ME 03904-0006
Tel: (207) 439-0922 Fax: (207) 439-8202
Web: www.kkorchid.com
Equipment for windowsill and "under lights" grower.

R.F. Orchids, Inc.
28100 SW 182 Avenue
Homestead, FL 33030-1804
Tel: (305) 245-4570 Fax: (305) 247-6568
Website: www.rforchids.com
Vandaceous and worm-growing species.

The Rod McLellan Company
914 S. Claremont Street, San Mateo, CA 94402
Toll-Free: 1-800-467-2443
Tel: (650) 373-3920 Fax: (650) 373-3913
Website: www.rodmclellan.com
Phalaenopsis, dendrobium, oncidium, paphiopedilum, cattleya, brassia, miltonia, and zygopetalum.

Santa Barbara Orchid Estate
1250 Orchid Drive, Santa Barbara, CA 93111
Tel: (805) 967-1284 Fax: (805) 683-3405
Website: www.sborchid.com
Species, cymbidium and lycaste hybrids.

Zuma Canyon Orchids
5949 Bonsall Drive, Malibu, CA 90465
Tel: (310) 457-9771 Fax: (310) 457-4783
Website: www.zumacanyonorchids.com
Phalaenopsis.

PUBLICATIONS

Orchid Digest
PO Box 1216, Redlands, CA 92373-0402
Tel: (909) 793-1536 Fax: (909) 793-9240
Web: www.orchiddigest.org

Orchid Review
RHS Subscription Service
PO Box 38, Ashford, Kent TN25 6PR
United Kingdom
Publication of the Royal Horticultural Society.

Orchid Research Newsletter
The Royal Botanic Gardens, Kew
Richmond, Surrey, TW9 3AB
United Kingdom
Tel: +44 (208) 940-1171
Fax: +44 (208) 332-5197

SOCIETIES

American Orchid Society
6000 South Olive Avenue,
West Palm Beach, FL 33405
Tel: (561) 585-8666 Fax: (561) 585-0654
Web: www.theaos.org OR orchidweb.org
Membership starts at US$40. Publishes AOS Orchids, Awards Quarterly and Lindleyana. Website includes worldwide Orchid Source Directory.

Canadian Orchid Congress
Society of provincial and regional orchid societies. Check website www.chebucto.ns.ca/Recreation/Orchid SNS/coc.html *for information.*

Glossary

Aerial root One having no contact with the ground or growing medium.

Air capacity Air-filled pore space. The percentage of the volume of potting medium that contains air after it has been saturated with water and allowed to drain.

Albino An orchid plant lacking the genetic ability to produce red-purple pigments, resulting in only white, green or yellow color in the flowers.

Backbulb An old, leafless pseudobulb.

Chromosomes Rod-like structures of the cell nucleus, occurring in pairs, that carry the genes and are involved in the transmission of hereditary characteristics.

Clone Group of plants produced vegetatively from one original seedling or stock and therefore containing identical genetic material.

Column The organ formed by the union of stamens, styles and stigmas.

Cross (1) To hybridize. (2) The progeny resulting from hybridization.

Cultivar In orchids has almost the same meaning as clone.

Deciduous A plant that sheds its leaves at a certain season.

Diploid Having two sets of chromosomes.

Epiphyte A plant that grows on another plant.

Fertilization (1) The conversion of ovules into seeds following pollination. (2) The provision of nutrients for the plant.

Foot-candle A measure of light intensity. 1 foot-candle = 10.8 lux.

Genetics The science of heredity.

Genus (pl. Genera) A closely related group of plants.

Grex The collective name given to the progeny of parents that are not of the same species.

Hybrid The offspring of a cross between parents that are genetically unlike.

Hybridization The act of producing hybrids by crossing one species or hybrid with another.

Intergeneric Between or among two or more genera.

Keiki A plantlet produced from the (usually an upper) node of a plant.

Labellum The third, and usually highly modified, unpaired petal of an orchid flower.

Lead A new vegetative growth.

Line breeding Raising successive generations usually of a single species.

Lip See labellum.

Lithophyte A plant growing on rocks; rupicolous.

Mericlone A plant produced in the laboratory by the culture of meristematic tissue.

Meristematic Undifferentiated tissue retaining the capacity for further growth, usually found in buds and growing points.

Monopodial A type of plant development in which the terminal bud of the stem continues its vegetative growth indefinitely.

Mycorrhiza A symbiotic relationship between plant roots and fungi.

Node The joint or point on a stem at which a leaf or bract is attached.

Ovary That part of the flower that develops into a seed pod.

Petals The two inner segments of an orchid flower, the third being the lip.

pH An expression of alkalinity with 7.0 representing neutral. Below is acidic, above alkaline.

Pod A mature ovary or seed capsule. The fruit of the orchid.

Pollination The act of placing pollen on the stigma.

Pollinia Pollen grains bound together in waxy masses.

Polyploid Having more than two sets of chromosomes – triploid, etc.

Pseudobulb A thickened stem.

Rhizome The connecting stem between the pseudobulbs or upright growths from which roots are produced.

Seedling A plant raised from seed, particularly a young plant that has yet to flower.

Sepals The three outer segments of the flower and usually the only segments visible in the unopened bud.

Sheath A modified leaf enfolding and protecting new shoots or flower buds.

Species A group of plants (or animals) that may show inter-graduation among individual members but having common significant characteristics separating it from any other group.

Spike Used in this book to refer to any type of inflorescence, irrespective of the mode of flower-bearing.

Stigma The part that receives the pollen for fertilization – in orchids usually a sticky cavity found on the undersurface of the column end.

Stoma (pl. Stomata) The minute opening where gas exchange occurs between the leaf and the atmosphere.

Sub-tribe One of the natural divisions into which large tribes are sometimes divided.

Symbiosis The living together of dissimilar organisms with benefit to both.

Sympodial A growth habit in which new shoots arise from buds in the rhizome.

Synonym (syn) An alternative name, as when the same plant has been given two or more names.

Systemic Capable of being absorbed and transported through-out the plant, as in a systemic chemical.

Taxonomist A scientist concerned with classification and naming of plants and animals.

Terrestrial Growing in or on the ground.

Tetraploid Having four sets of chromosomes.

Tissue culture Growing cells and tissue in an aseptic nutrient medium with the objective of developing whole plants.

Transpiration The loss of water vapor through the leaves.

Tribe A group of related genera forming a natural division within a family.

Triploid Having three sets of chromosomes.

Variety (var) A population of species found growing in the wild and showing variation from the type species. Only a taxonomist can give a varietal name (which follows the species name and is written in italics).

Vegetative propagation Propagated other than by seed, e.g. by division or tissue culture.

Velamen The layers of spongy cells on the outside of the root.

Virus A sub-microscopic infectious organic particle associated with disease.

Index